Brooke

National 4 & 5
ADMINISTRATION & IT

For SQA 2019 and beyond

Course Notes

Kathryn Pearce and
Carol Ann Taylor

001/10102018

10 9 8 7 6 5 4 3 2

ISBN 9780008282103

Published by
Leckie
An imprint of HarperCollins*Publishers*
Westerhill Road, Bishopbriggs, Glasgow, G64 2QT
T: 0844 576 8126   F: 0844 576 8131
leckiescotland@harpercollins.co.uk   www.leckiescotland.co.uk

Special thanks to
Donna Cole (copyediting and proofreading)
Louise Robb (proofreading)
Delphine Lawrance (picture research)
Eilidh Proudfoot (content review)

A CIP Catalogue record for this book is available from the British Library.

Acknowledgements
We would like to thank the following for permission to reproduce their material:
page 2-3 photo © David Pirvu; page 12-13 photo © Creativemarc; page 32 photo © auremar;
page 32 photo © konstantynov; page 32 photo © sixninepixels; page 32 photo © Martin Novak;
page 33 photo © tristan tan; page 42 photo © sheelamohanachandran2010; page 50 photo ©
Vytautas Kielaitis / Shutterstock.com page 56 photo © Maksim Shmeljov; page 58 photo ©
Cienpies Design; page 64-65 photo © Denys Prykhodov; page 93 photo © lucadp

Microsoft Excel excerpts used with permission from Microsoft
Microsoft Word excerpts used with permission from Microsoft
Microsoft PowerPoint excerpts used with permission from Microsoft
Microsoft Publisher excerpts used with permission from Microsoft

Whilst every effort has been made to trace the copyright holders, in cases where this has been
unsuccessful, or if any have inadvertently been overlooked, the Publishers would gladly receive any
information enabling them to rectify any error or omission at the first opportunity.

About the authors
Carol Ann Taylor is a Business Education teacher at Duncanrig Secondary School in East Kilbride.
She has been a setter and Principal Assessor for Standard Grade Administration and is currently
working with the SQA on National 5 Administration & IT.

Kathryn Pearce has been teaching in Our Lady & St Patrick's High in Dumbarton since 1995. She has
been a setter and examiner for Standard Grade Administration since 2001 and is currently
working with the SQA on National 5 Administration & IT.

Printed and bound by CPI Group (UK) Ltd, Croydon, CR0 4YY

Introduction

UNIT 1 – Theory

UNIT 2 – IT Applications

Preparing for the Assignment and Question Paper

Answers

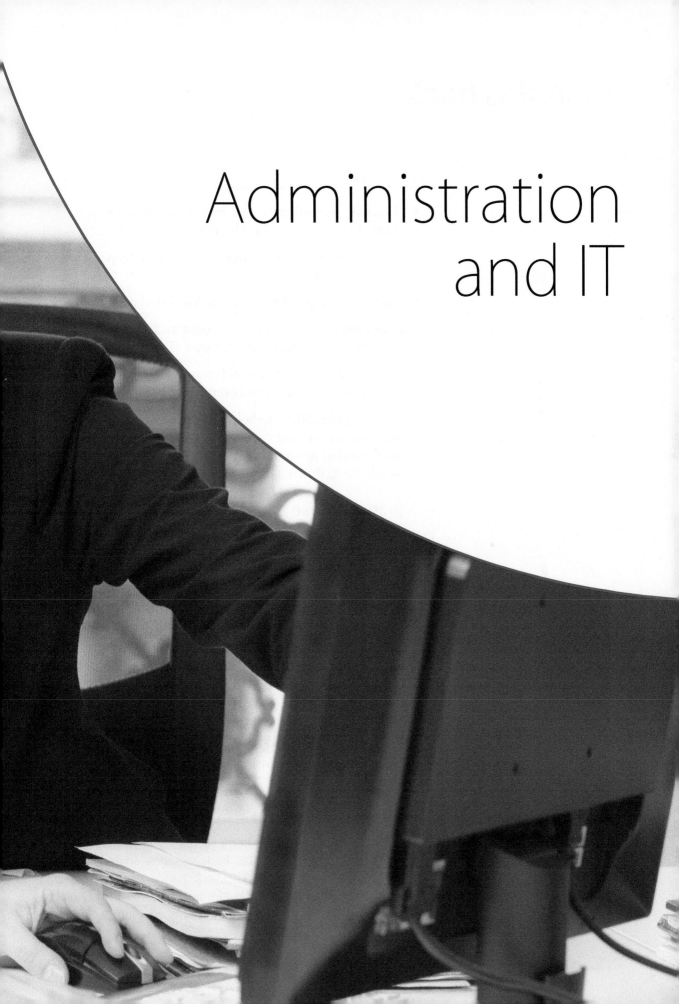

Administration and IT

About this book

You will find the following sections in this book:

- **Learning intentions** – an indication of what you are expected to learn in this chapter.

- **Watch points** – these provide suggestions to help complete tasks successfully.

- **Skills** – skills that the chapter helps you to develop.

- **Questions** – to test your knowledge and understanding of the course. Practical tasks test your IT skills.

- **Exam practice** – successful completion of these tasks shows that you have reached the required standard.

- **Learning checklist** – to help you determine which parts of the chapter you are confident with and which parts you may need to revise further. All the learning checklists are available to download from the Leckie & Leckie website.

Integrative course

In this course there will be an emphasis on skills development and the application of those skills. The course contains a significant practical element, which encourages the integration of skills, knowledge and understanding through practical activities.

While the skills, knowledge and understanding covered in this book help to develop and reflect current administrative practice, the course is flexible to take account of new technologies as they develop.

Software

This book is designed to be generic in nature and therefore does not contain step-by-step instructions for the use of specific software.

Resources to download

For many of the activities in this book you can download resources from the Leckie & Leckie website. To access these materials go to the page for this book on the Leckie & Leckie website (https://collins.co.uk/pages/scottish-curriculum-free-resources) and select the 'National 4 & 5 Administration and IT Course Notes – Second Edition' tab.

It is common practice in the SQA Assignment and Question Paper for instructions to be given in comments in the digital files. Comments must be **actioned** and **deleted** before the task is printed and submitted for marking. Failure to delete comments will result in the loss of a mark. Some comments may contain more than one instruction. You should make sure you have actioned all instructions before you delete the comment. Many of the tasks in the files that accompany this book make use of comments to allow you to become familiar with this process.

National 4

This book is designed to meet the requirements at National 5 level. However, much of the content is still appropriate for National 4 candidates. The National 4 course is still based on three units – Administrative Practices, IT Solutions for Administrators and Communication in Administration – whereas the revised National 5 course is now based on two areas of study – Theory and IT Applications.

In the Theory topics, National 4 candidates will focus on the responsibilities of **employees** whereas National 5 candidates will focus on the responsibilities of the **employer.** Additional skills are required at National 5 level for IT Applications. Further information on the differences between National 4 and National 5 levels can be found by visiting the National Qualifications page for Administration and IT on the SQA website (https://www.sqa.org.uk/sqa/45686.html).

> ### ⚠ Watch point
> You should know the difference between an employee and an employer – an employee is a person who works for an organisation in return for a wage/salary whereas an employer is a person or an organisation that employs an individual to carry out work for them and pays them a wage/salary.

Introduction

Why choose Administration and IT?

Administration supports the effective running of organisations across the economy, and offers wide-ranging employment opportunities. This course makes an important contribution to general education through developing a range of essential skills that will stand you in good stead regardless of the career path you eventually choose. It is also extremely useful in other walks of life. For example, being organised and being able to produce professional-looking documents could be extremely useful for producing coursework at college/university.

This course will develop your administrative and IT skills and will allow you to contribute to the effective working of an organisation.

The course – National 4

To pass the course at National 4 level you must pass all three of the units, as well as the Added Value Unit. These are all marked by your teacher. The Added Value Unit takes the form of an assignment, and its purpose is to draw on the knowledge, understanding and skills developed in the other three units. You will undertake practical administration- and IT-based tasks to organise and support a small-scale event or events.

The three units studied at National 4 level are:

- Administrative Practices
  The purpose of this unit is to give you a basic introduction to administration in the workplace. You will begin to appreciate important legislation affecting employees, key features of good customer service, and the skills, qualities and attributes required of administrators. The unit will also allow you to apply this basic understanding to carry out a range of straightforward administrative tasks required for organising and supporting small-scale events.

- IT Solutions for Administrators
  The purpose of this unit is to develop your basic skills in IT and organising and processing simple information in familiar administration-related contexts. You will use the following IT applications: word-processing, spreadsheets and databases to create and edit simple business documents. The unit will allow emerging technologies to be incorporated in order to ensure that its content remains current and relevant.

- Communication in Administration
  The purpose of this unit is to allow you to use IT for gathering and sharing simple information with others in familiar administration-related contexts. You will develop a basic understanding of what constitutes a reliable source of information and an ability to use appropriate methods for gathering information. You will also become able to communicate simple information in ways that show a basic awareness of its context, audience and purpose. The unit will allow emerging technologies to be incorporated in order to ensure that its content remains current and relevant.

The Course – National 5

Following a review of the National 5 course, the Unit Assessment element has been removed and the course now consists of two areas of study: Theory and IT Applications.

To pass the course at National 5 level you will sit an Assignment that is marked by an SQA marker. You will then sit a Question Paper during the exam diet (May/June) that is also marked by an SQA marker. You will be awarded a grade from A to D based on your total mark across these two assessments.

Component	Number of marks available	Duration
Question Paper	50	2 hours
Assignment	70	3 hours

Question Paper
The question paper gives you the opportunity to demonstrate:

- using IT functions in spreadsheet and database applications to produce and process information
- problem-solving
- administration theory

Marks are awarded for demonstrating the use of different IT applications and theory of administration in the workplace. Of the marks allocated, 14–26% are awarded for administration theory.

All questions **must** be attempted and you must work through them in the order presented. Questions are sampled from the 'Skills, knowledge and understanding' listed in the course specification.

A to-do list is provided to help you submit the correct printouts.

The following table shows the distribution and variances that are applied to each question when allocating marks.

Area of course	Mark allocation
Spreadsheet	20 marks, with a variance of +/– 3 marks
Database	20 marks, with a variance of +/– 3 marks
Theory	10 marks, with a variance of +/– 3 marks
Total	**50 marks**

Assignment

You will work through a series of planning, support and follow-up tasks related to an event or business.

The assignment gives you the opportunity to demonstrate:

- skills in using IT functions in word-processing, desktop publishing and presentations to produce and process information
- skills in using technology for investigation
- skills in using technology for electronic communication
- skills in problem-solving
- administration theory

Marks are awarded for demonstrating the use of different IT applications and theory of administration in the workplace. Of the marks allocated, 10–18% are awarded for administration theory, which is integrated within the tasks.

All tasks **must** be attempted and you must work through them in the order presented.

A to-do list is provided to help you submit the correct printouts.

The following table shows the distribution and variances that are applied to the tasks when allocating marks.

Area of course	Mark allocation
Word-processing/desktop publishing	30 marks, with a variance of +/– 3 marks
Communication (presentation, e-mail, e-diary, Internet)	30 marks, with a variance of +/– 3 marks
Theory	10 marks, with a variance of +/– 3 marks
Total	**70 marks**

National 5 command words

Command words are used to convey the level of detail required in a theory answer.

- **Outline** – give a brief sketch of content. This means more than simply naming but does not require a detailed description.
- **Describe** – give an account that shows understanding of a statement or concept. You should outline the concept **and** give an example/explanation or expansion. Two points are required to gain one mark.
- **Explain** – give details of **how** and **why** something is as it is. Two points are required to gain one mark.

> ⚠ **Watch point**
>
> Highlight the command word in a question and ensure your answer includes the detail required by that command word in order to maximise your marks!

Other skills

Throughout all three units (National 4) / two areas of study (National 5) you will also develop skills in the areas shown below:

- **Numeracy**
  - Information handling
- **Employability, enterprise and citizenship**
  - Employability
  - Information and communication technology (ICT)

- **Thinking skills**
  - Remembering
  - Understanding
  - Applying

Course progression

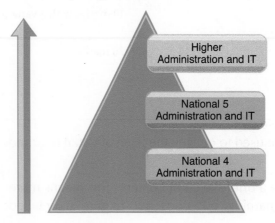

1
Theory

1 Tasks (duties) and skills/qualities of administrators

In this chapter you will learn about:

- The tasks (duties) of administrators.
- The skills/qualities of administrators.

Tasks (duties) of administrators

Administration helps any organisation run efficiently and in an organised way. The role of an administrator is therefore very important. An administrator will be required to fulfil a range of general administrative duties, such as receiving and sending e-mail, answering telephone enquiries, maintaining records, and so on. The range of tasks will depend on the size and type of organisation. For example, in a small organisation the administrator may be required to 'cover' reception, distribute mail, etc, whereas a large organisation will have specialist staff and departments to carry out these tasks.

The following diagram illustrates some of the tasks that may be expected of an administrator.

> ⚠ **Watch point**
>
> Duties will be found in the job description.

Sample answers to exam questions

Question: Outline the duties of an administrator.	Question: Describe the duties of an administrator.
An administrator will answer the telephone.	An administrator will answer the phone politely at all times and deal with any enquiries.
An administrator will update databases.	An administrator will create and update databases containing records of employees, customers or even suppliers.
An administrator will update spreadsheets.	An administrator will create and update spreadsheets on costings, wages, profit statements etc for the Finance department or sales figures for the Sales department.
An administrator will organise events/meetings.	An administrator will organise events/meetings by booking venues/rooms and ordering refreshments.
An administrator will organise business trips.	An administrator will organise business trips by booking appropriate travel tickets and accommodation.
An administrator will file documents.	An administrator will file documents – whether manual or electronic – in the correct order.

⚠ **Watch point**

You must make sure that your answer is appropriate to the command word used in the question.

Skills/qualities of an administrator

A skill is the ability to do something well, either through practising it or by gaining knowledge (training) in the skill, for example IT skills. A quality is a characteristic of a person, for example a good communicator, organised.

Skills/qualities include the following:

- organised
- able to communicate well
- able to work in a team
- co-operative
- willing to learn or develop
- able to multitask
- able to follow instructions
- able to demonstrate good IT skills

- patient
- tactful/discreet
- approachable

Sample answers to exam questions

> **Question: Explain the skills/qualities required by an administrator.**
>
> Administrators should be reliable/responsible/hard working *to ensure all tasks are completed on time.*
>
> Administrators should have good IT skills *because their job requires them to use spreadsheets, databases and word-processing software, as well as send and receive e-mails.*
>
> Administrators should be keen to learn *because IT skills constantly need updating.*

Finding the right person for the job

When an organisation is looking to appoint a new member of staff, they will draw up a **job description** and a **person specification**.

Job description

Details relating to a specific job are usually found in a job description. This sets out some background to the post, the duties/tasks associated with the post, the post holder's responsibilities and who their line manager is. It will also provide information on the hours to be worked, the salary to be paid and the holiday entitlement.

A job applicant uses this document to decide if the job is right for them.

Person specification

From the job description, the organisation can prepare a person specification. The roles and responsibilities detailed in the job description will highlight the skills, qualifications, experience and personal qualities required from a suitable candidate.

Each component of the person specification is usually classed as essential (a must-have skill or quality) or desirable (having this skill or quality would be an advantage, but it is not vital). Thus, a profile of the ideal candidate can be prepared and used to assist in the selection process.

A job applicant uses this document to decide if they have the necessary skills, qualifications, experience and personal qualities to be able to apply for the job.

A sample person specification for an administrator is shown below.

⚠ Watch point

Qualities/skills will be found in the person specification.

Administrator – person specification		
	Essential	**Desirable**
Skills, knowledge and abilities	• Ability to accurately key in data. • Ability to create and edit word-processed documents. • Ability to create and edit spreadsheets. • Confidence at using e-mail and the Internet. • Ability to file accurately. • Ability to organise small-scale events.	• Ability to create and edit databases. • Knowledge of prioritising workloads in order to meet deadlines. • Ability to learn new IT skills quickly.
Qualifications	• National 4/5 Administration and IT	• National 5 English and Maths
Experience		• Previous administrative experience at a junior level.
Personal qualities	• Ability to quickly follow verbal and written instructions. • Motivated and keen to learn. • Can use own initiative or work as part of a team. • Dependable/reliable.	• Organised. • Good at time management.

? Theory questions

1. Describe **two** tasks that would be carried out by an administrator.
2. Explain **two** skills/qualities required by an administrator.
3. Outline the purpose of a job description.
4. Outline the purpose of a person specification.

★ Exam practice

1. Download the file *Tasks and Skills EP1* from the Leckie and Leckie website.

   (a) Complete the task.

   (b) Insert your own name as a footer and print one copy of the completed task.

2. Download the file *Tasks and Skills EP2* from the Leckie and Leckie website.

   (a) Complete the task.

   (b) Insert your own name as a footer and print one copy of the completed task.

Skill

- Literacy
- Employability
- Skills for learning, life and work

Skills, knowledge and understanding	Strength ☺	☺	Weakness ☹	Next steps
Tasks (duties) of administrators				
I understand the tasks (duties) of an administrator: • creating and updating spreadsheets, databases, presentations, word-processing and desktop publishing documents • booking meeting rooms and venues • organising travel and accommodation arrangements • organising and storing files in the correct order				– Refer to instructions – Complete additional tasks – Ask teacher for help
Skills/qualities of administrators				
I understand the skills/qualities of administrators: • organised • able to communicate well • able to work in a team • co-operative • willing to learn or develop • able to multitask • able to follow instructions • able to demonstrate good IT skills • patient • tactful/discreet • approachable				– Refer to instructions – Complete additional tasks – Ask teacher for help

2 Customer service

In this chapter you will learn about:

- The key features of good customer service.
- The benefits of good customer service.
- The consequences of poor customer service.

The key features of good customer service

Customer service is sometimes seen to be more important for some employees than others, but it is equally important in all areas of the organisation. For example:

- A receptionist or any employee who deals directly with customers should have customer service as a key consideration in their job description and training.

- An administrator responsible for processing business documents may have little direct contact with customers, but customer satisfaction will be low if the documents contain errors.

Customer service policy

A customer service policy is a written statement of the organisation's policy and their plans for dealing with their customers. This document is produced to ensure that customers get:

- the product/service they want
- the standard they want
- a price that is acceptable

An organisation must aim to keep customers satisfied and ensure that all customers are treated in a consistent, fair way. A customer service policy will document the organisation's policy and how they will deal with the following aspects of customer service.

- Communicating with customers:
  - Employees should respond to customer letters or e-mails promptly.
  - Employees should answer the phone politely and within an agreed number of rings.

- – Employees should keep the customer informed at all times of up-to-date information and/or any changes to the agreement.

- Ensuring the quality of customer service:
  - – The organisation should provide regular customer service training for employees.
  - – The organisation should provide employees with a copy of the customer service policy.
  - – The organisation should regularly review the customer service policy.

- Monitoring that customer needs are satisfied:
  - – The organisation should survey their customers' opinions (this could be done online, by phone or by post).
  - – The organisation could use a mystery shopper to measure satisfaction.
  - – The organisation could analyse loyalty card use (frequency, types of products).

- Dealing with customer complaints.
  - – Employees should follow a formal procedure for dealing with all complaints.
  - – Organisations should use complaints as a learning experience, in order to not repeat the same mistakes.

Many organisations use their website to inform customers and potential customers about their customer service policy.

Mission statement

Most organisations have a mission statement, which gives an outline of the main intentions of the organisation. It can be a mix between a slogan and a summary of the organisation's aims. It is used to tell customers about the organisation and its ideals. It is also used to give employees an idea or vision of what the organisation hopes to achieve and helps them to focus their work towards achieving this goal.

Most mission statements are very short – usually no longer than two or three sentences.

⚠ Watch point

If an exam question asks how an organisation provides customer care you should outline/describe the features of good customer care.

The features of good customer service

Good customer service is about satisfying the needs of individuals and retaining their loyalty to the organisation.

Good customer service is essential if an organisation wants to survive in the market place, remain competitive, keep loyal customers and attract new customers.

The key features of good customer service are:

- using customer feedback forms
- providing all staff with a customer service policy statement
- putting the customer first
- communicating with customers effectively
- ensuring that all staff are knowledgeable about products and services being offered to customers
- ensuring all customer queries and problems are dealt with quickly and politely
- monitoring staff performance
- hiring suitable, friendly and helpful staff
- setting/evaluating staff targets
- providing a good after-sales service
- dealing with complaints effectively

The benefits of good customer service

It is important that all customers are treated well, as this will provide benefits for the organisation as well as the customer.

Satisfied customers	If customers are happy with the products or services being provided they will return and recommend the organisation to others.
Keeping loyal customers	This can be done by offering customer loyalty schemes, such as the Boots Advantage Card, Nectar points, etc.
Attracting new customers	This might be as a result of a recommendation from an existing customer or persuasion through loyalty schemes or advertising.
Satisfied and motivated employees	A clear customer service strategy allows employees to deal with all customers effectively, reducing stress and reducing staff absence/turnover.
Lower staff turnover/ less absenteeism	Employees are not stressed and will stay with the organisation. Employees are also less likely to take time off work if they are motivated and not stressed.
Reduced costs	The cost of recruiting new employees is not necessary.
Good/improved reputation	Recommendations from existing customers will improve the image of the organisation; if a customer has had a good experience with an organisation, they are likely to talk about it.
Competitive edge	A good reputation and/or more effective performance will mean that customers are more likely to choose that organisation rather than a competitor, therefore increasing market share.
Increased sales/profits	More customers (loyal and new) will mean that the organisation will increase the value of their sales and therefore increase their profit.
Fewer complaints	If customers are satisfied with the level of service there will be fewer complaints, resulting in staff who are more satisfied/motivated.
Improved efficiency/ increased productivity	If employees are motivated (because they do not have to deal with frequent customer complaints), they will work harder and complete more tasks. Less time spent dealing with customer complaints means they will get more work completed, i.e. productivity will be increased.
Reduced waste	Motivated employees will produce goods of a high standard, meaning that returns are less likely, which in turn reduces wastage. Motivated employees are also less likely to make mistakes, again resulting in less wastage.

Increased sales and/or profits will result from any of the other benefits of good customer service. For example, attracting new customers will lead to an increase in sales and therefore profits.

The impact of poor customer service

Customer service is important at all levels in an organisation. A business cannot survive without customers. In the same way that good customer service benefits an organisation, poor customer service will have a negative effect.

⚠ Watch point
Make sure you can identify/describe/explain **three** benefits of good customer service.

Dissatisfied customers	If customers are unhappy about the products or services being provided, they will not return and will tell others of their dissatisfaction.
Loss of customers	Dissatisfied customers will look for products or services elsewhere.
Bad publicity	Dissatisfied customers will talk, and leave bad reviews!
Demotivated employees	Employees who do not receive appropriate customer service training, or have not been advised of the organisation's customer service strategy, may make mistakes, not deal with customers effectively, and this will lead to stress.
Higher staff turnover/ more absenteeism	Unhappy employees will leave to work elsewhere.
Increased costs	The costs of recruiting/training new staff will be high.
Poor reputation	The organisation will gain a poor reputation through bad publicity and customers/employees talking of their dissatisfaction/ demotivation.
Poor competitive edge	Customers will be more likely to choose a competitor as they are performing more effectively.
Decreased sales/profits	Fewer customers (the loss of loyal customers and not attracting new customers) will result in lower sales and therefore lower profits.
Legal action	Employees not complying with consumer legislation may lead to customers taking legal action.
Increased customer complaints	If customers are dissatisfied with the service they receive, they will make complaints, leading to dissatisfied/demotivated employees.
Decreased market share	Dissatisfied customers will take their business elsewhere.
Lower efficiency/ decreased productivity	If employees need to deal with customer complaints, they will have less time to complete their core tasks, i.e. the tasks they are employed to complete. This can lead to reduced productivity (because less work is being done by employees).
Increased waste	If employees are not motivated, they are more likely to make mistakes when producing goods. Goods that are not completed to a high standard cannot be sold to customers, which will increase wastage and costs for the business.

> ⚠ **Watch point**
>
> A **consequence** is what happens **because** of poor customer service.

> ⚠ **Watch point**
>
> Make sure you can identify/ describe/explain **three** consequences of poor customer service.

Any one of the above could lead to the organisation ceasing to exist.

Decreased sales/profits will result from any of the other effects of poor customer service. For example, losing loyal customers will lead to a decrease in sales and therefore profits. A consequence of losing loyal customers is a decrease in sales/ profits.

❓Theory questions

1. Describe **three** features of customer service.
2. Describe **three** benefits of good customer service to an organisation.
3. Explain **three** consequences of poor customer service to an organisation.

★ Exam practice

1. Download the file *Customer Service EP1* from the Leckie and Leckie website.
   (a) Complete the task.
   (b) Insert your own name as a footer and print one copy of the completed task.
2. Download the file *Customer Service EP2* from the Leckie and Leckie website.
   (a) Complete the task.
   (b) Insert your own name as a footer and print one copy of the completed task.

 Skill

- Literacy
- Employability
- Skills for learning, life and work

Learning Checklist

Skills, knowledge and understanding	Strength ☺		Weakness ☹	Next steps
Key features of good customer service				
I understand the key features of good customer service: • using customer feedback forms • providing all staff with a customer service policy statement • ensuring all staff know the products and services offered to customers • ensuring all customer queries and problems are dealt with quickly and politely • monitoring staff performance • hiring suitable, friendly and helpful staff • setting and evaluating staff targets • ensuring staff follow complaints procedures				– Refer to instructions – Complete additional tasks – Ask teacher for help

(continued)

Skills, knowledge and understanding	Strength ☺	Weakness ☹		Next steps

Benefits of good customer service

| I understand the benefits of good customer service:
• customer loyalty
• reduced complaints
• increased profits/sales and decreased costs
• good publicity
• lower staff turnover/less absenteeism
• competitive edge, leading to increased market share
• improved efficiency/increased productivity
• reduced waste | | | | – Refer to instructions
– Complete additional tasks
– Ask teacher for help |

Consequences of poor customer service

| I understand the consequences of poor customer service:
• increased customer complaints
• decreased profits/sales and increased costs
• negative publicity
• higher staff turnover/more absenteeism
• decreased market share/fewer customers
• lower efficiency/decreased productivity
• increased waste | | | | – Refer to instructions
– Complete additional tasks
– Ask teacher for help |

3 Health and safety

In this chapter you will learn about:

- Key organisational responsibilities in terms of health and safety, for example:
  - the use of induction training to cover health and safety issues
  - understanding what employers must do to observe health and safety rules, in accordance with current legislation
  - the identification of hazards in the workplace to ensure safe practice, such as completing an accident report form
- Features of current legislation:
  - Health and Safety at Work etc Act 1974 (HASAWA)
  - fire safety
  - display screen equipment regulations
  - first aid
  - workplace regulations

Identification of hazards and measures to ensure safe practice

Accidents can occur within the workplace. It is important that all hazards are minimised in order to reduce the number of accidents that occur.

Major injuries can be caused by:

- slips or trips (from trailing cables, open filing cabinets, etc)
- falling (when trying to reach the top of a cupboard or shelf)
- poor lifting and handling techniques.

Common sense should prevail at all times. The following checklist could be used to remind employees of the common sense approach they should take towards health and safety. Notices should also be placed in appropriate areas to remind staff of their health and safety duties.

Safety checklist

To prevent slips or trips, employees should:	✓

• position desks to avoid trailing cables or use a cable management system
 	
   • position filing cabinets away from the door
 	
   • never store heavy materials in a hard-to-reach place (provide a step ladder if required)
 	
   • mop up any liquids that have been spilled (use a danger sign if the floor is still wet)
 	
   • keep passageways free from obstacles	

To prevent fires, employees should:	✓

• keep liquids away from computer equipment
 	
   • never overload power sockets (reposition furniture or install more power points if required)
 	
   • report any faults immediately
 	
   • empty waste bins regularly
 	
   • smoke only in designated areas
 	
   • never prop open fire doors	

General warnings:	✓

• Never attempt to fix equipment unless fully trained to do so.
 	
   • Report loose flooring.
 	
   • Employees should always keep their own work areas tidy.	

If an accident does occur within the organisation, an **accident report form** and an **accident book** must be completed. The accident report form may be completed either by a witness to the accident or the person involved in the accident. Examples of an accident report form and an accident book are over the page.

Accident report form	
Name of injured person	Amy Taylor
Date of birth	16/9/88
Position in the organisation	Finance Manager
Date and time of incident	22 June 2018, 11 am
Brief description of accident (continue on separate sheet if required)	Tripped over trailing cables
Place of accident	Reception
Details of injury	Broken wrist, sprained ankle
First aid treatment (if given)	Ice pack on wrist and ankle
Was the injured person taken to hospital/doctor	Taken to Glasgow General Hospital – Accident and Emergency department
Name(s) and position(s) of person(s) present when accident occurred	Chloe Pearce, Human Resources Manager

Signature of person reporting the accident ....

Date ....

Accident book					
Date	Time	Location	Name of injured person	Witness	Details of accident and action taken
12/4/18	3.30 pm	Sales department	Kirstin Dolan	Lewis Smith	Fell whilst trying to reach material on high shelf. Head bandaged and taken to hospital.
22/6/18	11 am	Reception	Amy Taylor	Chloe Pearce	Tripped over trailing cables. Ice pack placed on wrist and ankle. Taken to hospital.

The accident report form and accident book may be stored on the organisation's internal computer network (Intranet), which would allow employees to access it, complete it on the computer and e-mail it immediately to the relevant person.

It is very important that the organisation maintains a record of all accidents – if there are too many accidents occurring then the Health and Safety Executive will investigate health and safety practices within the firm.

Health and safety policy statement

An organisation that employs five or more people must, by law, have a written health and safety policy. Describing how the organisation will manage health and safety lets staff and others know that the organisation is committed to keeping all staff healthy and safe. The policy should include the following information:

- The name of the person(s) responsible for carrying out health and safety checks within the organisation – and how often this will occur.

- Appropriate health and safety training to be given to employees.

- The organisation's evacuation procedure.

- How often employees will be consulted on day-to-day health and safety conditions.

- Details of the maintenance of equipment.

The Health and Safety at Work Act 1974 states that all employees must have access to the organisation's health and safety policy. The policy may be stored on the organisation's Intranet to ensure ease of access by all employees, this also make the regular updating of the policy easier, as organisations must review and revise their policy as often as necessary.

Organisations may provide employees with a copy of their health and safety policy during their **induction training**. Health and safety procedures will be explained in detail during induction training, and, evacuation and first-aid procedures will also be explained.

⚠ Watch point

A policy statement is a document that explains procedures carried out by an organisation, i.e. how things are done.

⚠ Watch point

Induction training is training given to **new** employees to introduce them to the organisation.

Current legislation

Health and Safety at Work Act 1974

Responsibilities of an employee	Responsibilities of an employer (organisation)
• Employee should **take** reasonable care of their own health and safety and the health and safety of others. • Employee should **co-operate** with the employer on health and safety matters. • Employee should **not misuse** or interfere with anything that is provided for employees' health and safety. • Employee should **report** any accidents or hazards immediately to their employer.	• Employer/organisation should **provide** and maintain suitable surroundings for employees such as lighting, workstations etc. • Employer/organisation should **provide** information and training on all health and safety matters and requirements and ensure that employees adhere to these. • Employer/organisation should **provide** protective clothing and equipment, if necessary, and make sure that all equipment and machinery is checked and tested on a regular basis. • Employer/organisation should **prepare** a health and safety policy to be given to all employees and update it on a regular basis. • Employer/organisation should **ensure** an accident report form and accident book are kept and maintained. The employer should also make sure staff are aware that all accidents/incidents are to be recorded by including this in induction training/notices etc.

Health and Safety (Display Screen Equipment) Regulations 1992

This act is designed to minimise the potential risks associated with the use of visual display units (VDUs), including:

Eye strain

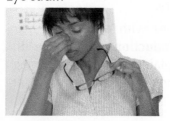

Headaches

Repetitive strain injury

Backache

Responsibilities of an employee	Responsibilities of an employer (organisation)
Avoid potential health hazards by: • Making use of adjustment facilities for the VDU. • Adjusting chair for maximum comfort. • Arranging desk and screen to avoid glare.	• Assess workstation requirements. • Provide adjustable seating. • Provide adjustable and tilting screens. • Provide health and safety training for employees. • Organise daily work of VDU users so that there are regular rest breaks or changes in activity.

Health and Safety (First Aid) Regulations 1981

Employers are required to:

- provide a well-stocked first aid box
- appoint a first aider (it is recommended that there should be one for every 50–100 employees)
- inform staff of first aid procedures
- keep a record of all accidents/incidents

Fire Precautions (Places of Work) Regulations 1995

Employers are required to:

- assess fire risks in the organisation
- provide appropriate fire-fighting equipment such as fire extinguishers
- check and maintain fire-fighting equipment
- provide warning systems (and check them regularly)
- train employees in fire procedures
- regularly check evacuation procedures (regular fire drills would help check that routes are appropriate, timings are acceptable, etc)

Reporting of Injuries, Diseases and Dangerous Occurrences Regulations 1995 (RIDDOR)

Employers are required to:

- record any accident, occupational disease or dangerous occurrence that requires reporting under RIDDOR
- record any other occupational accident causing injuries that result in a worker being away from work or incapacitated for more than three consecutive days
- produce RIDDOR records when asked by Health and Safety Executive or local authority inspectors

⚠ Watch point

Fire evacuation notices should be displayed prominently for all employees and visitors to see – they should be displayed in all areas, including the reception area.

33

? Theory questions

1. Outline **two** ways the following pieces of legislation are being breached in the picture above.

   (a) Health and Safety at Work Act 1974

   (b) Health and Safety (Display Screen Equipment) Regulations 1992

2. State what is meant by the term **induction training**.

3. Complete the following table with the responsibilities of an employer and an employee with regard to the Health and Safety at Work Act 1974. The first one has been completed for you.

Responsibilities of an employee	Responsibilities of an employer (organisation)
Employee should **take** reasonable care of their own health and safety and the health and safety of others.	Employer/organisation should **provide** and maintain suitable surroundings for employees such as lighting, workstations etc.

4. Identify **two** responsibilities of an employee and an employer stated in the Health and Safety (Display Screen Equipment) Regulations 1992.

5. Outline the responsibilities of an organisation that are required by the Health and Safety (First Aid) Regulations 1981.

6. Suggest **two** steps that should be taken to prevent injury from fire within an organisation.

★ **Exam practice**

1. Download the file *Health and Safety EP1* from the Leckie and Leckie website.
   (a) Complete the task.
   (b) Insert your name as a footer and print one copy of the completed task.
2. Download the file *Health and Safety EP2* from the Leckie and Leckie website.
   (a) Complete the task.
   (b) Insert your name as a footer and print one copy of the completed task.

Ψ Skill

- Literacy
- Communication
- Information technology
- Presentation
- Employability
- Skills for learning, life and work

Learning Checklist

Skills, knowledge and understanding	Strength ☺	☹	Weakness ☹	Next steps
Features of current legislation				
I understand the features of current legislation: • the Health and Safety at Work etc Act 1974 (HASAWA) • fire safety • display screen equipment (DSE) regulations • first aid • workplace regulations				– Refer to instructions – Complete additional tasks – Ask teacher for help
Key organisational responsibilities in terms of health and safety				
I understand the key organisational responsibilities in terms of health and safety: • the use of induction training to cover health and safety issues • understanding what employers must do to observe health and safety rules, in accordance with current legislation • the identification of hazards in the workplace and measures to ensure safe practice, such as completing an accident report form				– Refer to instructions – Complete additional tasks – Ask teacher for help

4 Security of people, property and information

In this chapter you will learn about:

- Key employee and organisational responsibilities in terms of security of people.
- Key employee and organisational responsibilities in terms of security of property.
- Key employee and organisational responsibilities in terms of security of information.
- Features of current legislation, such as General Data Protection Regulations (GDPR), the Computer Misuse Act 1990 and the Copyright, Designs and Patents Act 1988.

⚠ Watch point

If a question asks how the organisation could ensure the security of people, property or information use a verb in your answer to illustrate what the organisation is actually doing.

Security of people

Sample answers to exam questions

Both questions include the command word **explain** so you need to give two points to gain one mark. The text in italic shows the second point you need to make – the **why** part of the explanation.

Question: Explain the responsibilities of employees in terms of security of people.	Question: Explain the responsibilities of employers (organisations) in terms of security of people.
Employee should **wear** their name badge at all times *to ensure that any intruders are easily identified.*	Employer/organisation should **install** intercom/swipe cards/keypads/iris/fingerprint recognition *to prevent unauthorised entry to the premises.*
Employee should **wear** uniforms provided by the organisation *as this makes unauthorised visitors easily identifiable.*	Employer/organisation should **employ** security guards *to prevent unauthorised access.*
Employee should **ensure** their visitors report to and sign in at reception *to prevent unauthorised entry to the premises.*	Employer/organisation should **install** CCTV *to monitor secure areas.*
	Employer/organisation should **provide** all staff and visitors with ID badges *so that unauthorised visitors can be identified.*
	Employer/organisation should **provide** uniforms for staff *so that members of staff can be easily identified.*
	Employer/organisation should **provide** a reception area *to monitor visitors to the organisation.*
	Employer/organisation should **install** panic alarms *to provide reassurance to staff working in isolated areas.*

Security of property

In addition to the measures mentioned above regarding security of people, the following measures could also be taken to ensure the security of property.

Sample answers to exam questions

Both questions include the command word **explain** so you need to give two points to gain one mark. The text in italic shows the second point you need to make – the **why** part of the explanation.

Question: Explain the responsibilities of employees in terms of security of property.	Question: Explain the responsibilities of employers (organisations) in terms of security of property.
Employee should **ensure** that all office doors and windows are locked before leaving the premises *to prevent unauthorised entry to the premises.*	Employer/organisation should **attach** equipment to desks, for example computers, keyboards etc can be bolted to desks *to ensure no one can remove them from the premises.*
Employee should **lock away** any portable equipment when not in use *to prevent it being stolen.*	Employer/organisation should **keep** a list of equipment (including serial numbers) *to allow equipment to be identified. This may act as a deterrent to thieves.*
Employee should **set** the alarm before leaving if they are the last person on the premises *to deter unauthorised entry.*	Employer/organisation should **provide** security cables to be used with portable items such as laptops/notebooks/netbooks etc. *This will secure items to ensure they cannot be removed from the premises.*
	Employer/organisation should **employ** security guards *to prevent unauthorised access to premises.*
	Employer/organisation should **mark** equipment with UV (ultraviolet) pens *so that it can be identified by police in the event that it is stolen. This may act as a deterrent to thieves.*
	Employer/organisation should **install** locks on doors and windows *to prevent theft.*
	Employer/organisation should **provide** staff with lockers *to prevent loss of personal property.*

Security of information

Sample answers to exam questions

Both questions include the command word **explain** so you need to give two points to gain one mark. The text in italic shows the second point you need to make – the **why** part of the explanation.

⚠ **Watch point**

Information may be paper-based (manual) or electronic (on computer).

Question: Explain the responsibilities of employees in terms of security of information.	Question: Explain the responsibilities of employers (organisations) in terms of security of information.
Employee should **change** their passwords regularly *to prevent unauthorised editing/viewing of files.*	Employer/organisation should **issue** all staff who access the computer system with a username and password *to control the use of the system and prevent unauthorised access.*
Employee should **only use** files/pen drives etc from reliable sources *to prevent viruses getting in to the computer system.*	Employer/organisation should **set up** appropriate access rights for employees *so that only authorised staff can view information.*
Employee should **lock** their computer if they are away from their desk for a period of time/activate a password-protected screensaver *to ensure unauthorised personnel cannot access information.*	Employer/organisation should **train** staff to put passwords on files *to prevent unauthorised editing/viewing of files.*

(continued)

Question: Explain the responsibilities of employees in terms of security of information.	Question: Explain the responsibilities of employers (organisations) in terms of security of information.
	Employer/organisation should **provide** locks on filing cabinets *to ensure only authorised staff can access the files in them.*
	Employer/organisation should **ensure** a backup is made of all files *so that a copy is available if data is lost/damaged/corrupted.*
	Employer/organisation should **set up** a system whereby employees are prompted to change their password regularly *to prevent unauthorised editing/viewing of files.*
	Employer/organisation should **purchase/install** anti-virus software *to ensure files are protected from viruses.*
	Employer/organisation should **encrypt** files *to prevent unauthorised viewing/editing.*
	Employer/organisation should **ensure** confidential/important files are saved as read-only *so that only authorised staff can amend them.*

General Data Protection Regulations (GDPR)

GDPR is a Europe-wide set of data protection laws designed to ensure a consistent approach to data privacy practice across Europe. The emphasis is on protecting citizens and their data, and giving people more information about, and control over, how their personal data is used.

The GDPR apply to all organisations that use personal data.

The GDPR set out seven key principles of personal data privacy:

- **Lawfulness, fairness and transparency** – data should be processed lawfully, fairly and in a transparent manner in relation to individuals.

- **Purpose limitation** – data should be collected for specified, explicit and legitimate purposes and not further processed in a manner that is incompatible with those purposes.

- **Data minimisation** – data should be adequate, relevant and limited to what is necessary in relation to the purposes for which they are processed.

- **Accuracy** – data should be error-free and, where necessary, kept up to date; every reasonable step must be taken to ensure that personal data that is inaccurate is updated or deleted without delay.

- **Storage limitation** – data should be kept in a form that permits identification of data subjects for no longer than is necessary for the purposes for which the personal data are processed.

- **Integrity and confidentiality (security)** – data should be processed in a manner that ensures appropriate security of the personal data, including protection against unauthorised or unlawful processing and against accidental loss, destruction or damage, using appropriate technical or organisational measures.

- **Accountability –** This requires the organisation to take responsibility for what they do with personal data and how they comply with the other principles.

  An organisation must have appropriate measures and records in place to be able to demonstrate that they are complying with the GDPR.

Failure to comply with the principles may result in substantial fines. A fine of up to €20 million, or 4% of an organisation's total worldwide annual turnover, whichever is higher, may be imposed.

Computer Misuse Act 1990

The purpose of the Computer Misuse Act 1990 is to prohibit unlawful access to computer systems. This act makes it illegal to:

- access computers without permission (eg hacking)

- access computers with the intention of committing a criminal offence

- access computers to change or alter details without permission

Copyright, Designs and Patents Act 1988

This Act gives the authors or creators of a piece of work control over how their work is used and also ensures they receive credit and compensation when it is used. Music, books, videos and software can all be covered by copyright law.

The Act seeks to ensure that no unauthorised copying takes place. To copy or reproduce something that is covered by copyright law, permission must be sought from the copyright owner and a fee may need to be paid.

? Theory questions

1. How can keypads/combination locks/swipe cards restrict unauthorised access?
2. Describe **three** security measures taken by an organisation to ensure the security of people.
3. Describe **three** security measures taken by an organisation to protect property.
4. In what **two** ways can usernames and passwords restrict access to information?
5. Outline **three** other methods of protecting information held on computer.
6. Describe the main principles of the General Data Protection Regulations (GDPR).
7. Describe the purpose of the Computer Misuse Act 1990.
8. Describe the purpose of the Copyright, Designs and Patents Act 1988.

Skill

- Decision-making
- ICT
- Literacy
- Employability
- Skills for learning, life and work

★ Exam practice

1. Download the file *Security EP1* from the Leckie and Leckie website.
   (a) Complete the task.
   (b) Insert your name as a footer and print one copy of the completed task.
2. Download the file *Security EP2* from the Leckie and Leckie website.
   (a) Complete the task.
   (b) Insert your name as a footer and print one copy of the completed task.

Learning Checklist

Skills, knowledge and understanding	Strength ☺	☺	Weakness ☹	Next steps
Key organisational responsibilities in terms of security of people				
I understand the organisational responsibilities of security of people: • installing secure entry systems	✓			– Refer to instructions – Complete additional tasks – Ask teacher for help
Key organisational responsibilities in terms of security of property				
I understand the organisational responsibilities in terms of security of property: • applying security marking	✓			– Refer to instructions – Complete additional tasks – Ask teacher for help
Key organisational responsibilities in terms of security of information				
I understand the key organisational responsibilities in terms of security of information: • issuing usernames and passwords	✓			– Refer to instructions – Complete additional tasks – Ask teacher for help
Features of current legislation				
I understand the features of current legislation: • data protection • computer misuse • copyright	✓			– Refer to instructions – Complete additional tasks – Ask teacher for help

5 Sources of information from Internet

In this chapter you will learn about:

- Features of reliable Internet sources of information.
- The benefits of using reliable Internet sources of information.
- The consequences of using unreliable Internet sources of information.

The Internet

The **Internet** is a network of connected computers (computers linked together over a large geographical area – across the world). It is Wide Area Network (**WAN**).

The Internet has many uses for an organisation:

- Researching:
    - travel/accommodation information – availability, costs, etc
    - latest foreign travel advice
    - travel routes (for example, for salespeople)
    - latest travel information (accidents, traffic jams on routes, flight delays etc)
    - competitors' prices/promotions
    - potential supplier's deals

- latest news
- government publications
- Advertising the organisation's products and job vacancies.
- E-commerce (electronic commerce):
  - selling products online – this allows access to a global market, 24/7, which could increase the organisation's sales and profits
  - buying products from suppliers: prices, delivery dates and other factors can be compared before selecting the best deal
- Booking travel/hotel accommodation.
- Using e-mail to contact customers, suppliers etc
- Web conferencing: for face-to-face discussions by users in different locations.
- Gaining customer feedback and reviews.

⚠ Watch point

Always use a secure website, particularly if using a credit card or other method of payment over the Internet. A secure website will have a padlock sign at the end of the URL window or https at the start of the address to show that it is a verified website and uses encryption.

Features of reliable Internet sources of information

Non-biased	Using a range of websites will help achieve a balanced view before making any decisions. Many organisations use their website as a marketing tool and only include positive information – users should use a number of reliable websites to ensure they get a balanced view.
Complete/sufficient	Using a range of websites should ensure a user has enough information to make an informed decision.
Accurate	Users should always check information contained on a website is correct (see 'regularly updated site' and 'reliable' below).
Regularly updated site	Users should try to use websites that are updated on a regular basis – check the properties of a website for this information or look to see if some obvious up-to-date information is included on the website, such as 'today's special offers'. These websites are more likely to be accurate.
Good reputation of author	Users relying on the Internet for accurate information should only use websites that are reputable or from a well-known organisation, such as government websites.
Reliable	Users of the Internet must be selective about the sources of information they use. Anyone can create a website and post information, which may be inaccurate and therefore unreliable.
	Users should look carefully at the website – if the site looks poorly designed and substandard it has probably been created by an amateur and it is likely to be unreliable.

Benefits of using reliable Internet sources of information

- Information is usually up to date – many websites are updated on a regular basis to give the latest prices, availability etc, which makes decision-making more reliable.

- A vast range of information is available – this gives users access to much more information than they previously could have gathered, meaning the correct decision is more likely to be reached.

- An organisation will gain a good reputation if it makes good decisions for customers (good decisions have been made due to the fact it has used reliable information).

- If an organisation has access to up-to-date information, it may be able to take advantage of special offers, which would allow it to reduce its costs.

- Information is instantly available, for example when booking a flight a number of reputable websites could be searched for prices and availability, allowing the organisation to book the most appropriate flight. This would save the organisation time and money.

Consequences of using unreliable Internet sources of information

Using out-of-date information could have a damaging effect on a business, for example using an out-of-date train timetable could result in staff missing important meetings and thus losing orders/sales. Using out-of-date information is worse than having no information at all!

As anyone can post information on a website, it is important to check that it is accurate and free from bias (this is when someone puts their opinion/slant on the information and does not stick to fact). This could influence your results, for example if you are writing a report you may include inaccuracies and bias that could lead to wrong decisions being made.

If an organisation passes on unreliable information to its customers it may gain a bad reputation, which could lead to customers not using the business again in the future. This would result in lost sales and reduced profits.

Using unreliable Internet sources of information could also result in missed opportunities. For example, the organisation may be unaware of innovative product designs etc which customers may now demand – this could lead to the organisation losing sales.

❓Theory questions

1. Outline **three** features of reliable Internet sources of information.
2. Explain **three** benefits of using reliable Internet sources of information.
3. Explain **three** consequences of using unreliable Internet sources of information.

★ Exam practice

1. Download the file *Sources EP1* from the Leckie and Leckie website.
   (a) Complete the task.
   (b) Insert your name as a footer and print one copy of the completed task.
2. Download the file *Sources EP2* from the Leckie and Leckie website.
   (a) Complete the task.
   (b) Insert your name as a footer and print one copy of the completed task.

🌳 Skill

- Decision-making
- ICT
- Literacy
- Employability
- Skills for learning, life and work

Learning Checklist

Skills, knowledge and understanding	Strength ☺		Weakness ☹	Next steps
Features of reliable sources of internet information				
I understand the features of reliable sources of internet information • non-biased • complete/sufficient • accurate • regularly updated site • reputation of author				– Refer to instructions – Complete additional tasks – Ask teacher for help
Benefits of using reliable internet sources of information				
I understand the benefits of using reliable internet sources of information eg • good decisions can be made • organisation gains a good reputation • organisation gains opportunities				– Refer to instructions – Complete additional tasks – Ask teacher for help
Consequences of using reliable internet sources of information				
I understand the consequences of using reliable internet sources of information eg • missed meetings • wrong decisions can be made • organisation gets a bad reputation • organisation loses money • organisation loses opportunities				– Refer to instructions – Complete additional tasks – Ask teacher for help

6 File management

- Features of file management.
- The benefits of good file management.
- The consequences of poor file management.

What is file management?

File management is the method by which information is stored and organised. Good file management allows files to be found quickly, reducing time spent searching.

Features of a file management system

- Files should be saved using appropriate/meaningful names.
- Files should be saved into appropriately named folders.
- Files should be backed up on a regular basis.
- Files that are no longer required should be archived/ deleted.
- Anti-virus software should be updated on a regular basis.
- Passwords should be used to keep confidential files secure.

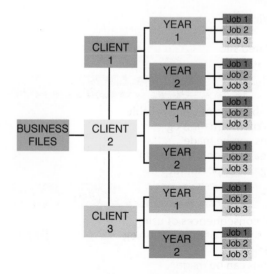

Benefits of good file management

- Employees do not have difficulty finding files, *which saves time.*
- Employees understand how files are saved, *which reduces frustration/stress.*
- Time is not wasted trying to locate files, *which leads to satisfied customers (who do not need to wait while information is found).*
- Efficiency is improved, *which leads to a better reputation.*
- Removing unnecessary/out-of-date files frees up computer storage, *which will speed up processing.*
- Files can be saved on a network, *which saves storage space (because there is no need for duplication of files).*
- Files can be saved on a network, *which means that duplication is not necessary and updating only needs to be done once.*
- Files are kept up to date/current, *which means that decisions are made based on the most up-to-date information.*
- Confidential files cannot be accessed by unauthorised personnel, *which means that data protection legislation is not breached.*

> **⚠ Watch point**
>
> To explain the benefits of good file management, your answer must say why it is a benefit – this can be done by using a phrase such as 'which means', 'to ensure' or 'so that'. You can see this in the italic text in this list.

Consequences of poor file management

- Time is wasted trying to find files, *which can lead to dissatisfied customers and staff becoming frustrated/ stressed.*
- Files are duplicated, *which wastes storage space on the network.*
- Efficiency levels are reduced, (as employees waste time searching for files and not carrying out their core tasks), *which can lead to a poor reputation for the organisation.*
- Duplicate files may not have been updated, *which means employees may be accessing out-of-date information.*
- Unauthorised personnel may access confidential files, *which could lead to legal action being taken against the organisation.*

❓ Theory questions

1. Outline **three** features of file management.
2. Explain **three** benefits of good file management.
3. Describe **three** consequences of poor file management.

1. Download the file *File Management EP1* from the Leckie and Leckie website.

    (a) Complete the task.

    (b) Insert your own name as a footer and print one copy of the completed task.

2. Download the file *File Management EP2* from the Leckie and Leckie website.

    (a) Complete the task.

    (b) Insert your own name as a footer and print one copy of the completed task.

Learning Checklist

Skills, knowledge and understanding	Strength ☺	☺	Weakness ☹	Next steps
Features of file management				
I understand the features of file management: • appropriately named files and folders • archiving/deleting old files • regular backups • regular antivirus updates • security on files				– Refer to instructions – Complete additional tasks – Ask teacher for help
Benefits of good file management				
I understand the benefits of good file management: • saves time finding files • saves storage space on network • less stress for employees looking for files • improved efficiency, leading to a good reputation • no duplication means that files are more likely to be up to date				– Refer to instructions – Complete additional tasks – Ask teacher for help
Consequences of poor file management				
I understand the consequences of poor file management: • wastes time finding files • wastes storage space on network • more stress for employees looking for files • lower efficiency, leading to a poor reputation • duplication, meaning files are less likely to be up to date				– Refer to instructions – Complete additional tasks – Ask teacher for help

7 Corporate image

- Features of corporate image.
- The benefits of having a corporate image.
- The consequences of not having a corporate image/having a negative corporate image.

Corporate image, or reputation, describes the manner in which a company, its activities and its products or services are perceived by outsiders.

Corporate image can be implemented through:

- policy statements
- training
- employing specialised staff
- having an effective recruitment and selection procedure

Features of corporate image

- **Standardised colours, fonts, graphics** – for example the use of red and blue in the Tesco brand the golden arches of McDonalds.

- **An easily recognisable logo** – for example the Tesco logo appears on all correspondence, signs etc

- **An easily recognisable slogan** – such as Tesco's 'Every little helps'. 'I'm lovin' it' is McDonald's global slogan which means the brand is recognised world-wide.

- **An easily recognisable uniform for all employees** – employees can be identified from the uniform/colours they wear.

- **A standardised store layout** – a similar layout is used across all branches. For example, all McDonald's restaurants look the same regardless of location.

- **Standardised responses to frequently asked questions (FAQs)** – customers recognise that all enquiries are dealt with in the same way across all branches.

- **Consistent presentation of IT documents/house style** – all documents issued by the organisation are consistent, professional and produced to the same high standards. This is an important tool to help build up a brand image.

Benefits of having a corporate image

- **An instantly recognisable brand** – this can be used as an effective promotional and marketing tool as it will help customers to remember the organisation. It gives the organisation a competitive edge (customers are more likely to choose an organisation they are aware of.

- **A professional reputation** – customers who are satisfied with an organisation's service will tell others and this can help to improve the reputation of the business. A good corporate brand establishes confidence, loyalty, trust and a stronger customer relationship. It also helps to attract new customers.

- **Consistency** – meaning that customers are dealt with fairly and as a result are likely to return to the organisation. Consistency can be implemented through policy statements, training, employing specialised staff and having an effective recruitment and selection procedure.

- **A valuable asset** – brand image is worth millions of pounds for many companies, which means the most valuable asset a company may have when being sold is not the premises it owns but the trademarks and brand image it has built up over the years.

Consequences of not having a corporate image/having a negative corporate image

- **No recognisable brand** – which puts the organisation at a disadvantage. Customers are more likely to choose a competitor, which means sales/profits will fall.

- **Less professional reputation** – meaning that customers could choose to go elsewhere. It also makes it more difficult to attract new customers.

- **Lack of consistency** – meaning that customers will feel they are not dealt with fairly. If they are unhappy/dissatisfied they will not return to the business, which will lead to lower sales and a poor reputation.

? Theory questions

1. Outline **four** features of corporate image.
2. Outline **two** ways an organisation can implement corporate image.
3. Explain **two** benefits of having a corporate image.
4. Explain **two** consequences of a negative corporate image.

⭐ **Exam practice**

1. Download the file *Corporate Image EP1* from the Leckie and Leckie website.

   (a) Complete the task.

   (b) Insert your own name as a footer and print one copy of the completed task.

2. Download the file *Corporate Image EP2* from the Leckie and Leckie website.

   (a) Complete the task.

   (b) Insert your own name as a footer and print one copy of the completed task.

Learning Checklist

Skills, knowledge and understanding	Strength 😊	😐	Weakness 🙁	Next steps
Features of corporate image				
I understand the features of corporate image: • standardised colours, fonts, graphics • logo • slogan • staff uniform • store layout • standardised responses to frequently asked questions (FAQs) • standardised customer service • consistent presentation of IT documents using a house style				– Refer to instructions – Complete additional tasks – Ask teacher for help
Benefits of having a corporate image				
I understand the benefits of having a corporate image: • instantly recognisable brand • professional reputation • staff are consistent, so customers are dealt with fairly				– Refer to instructions – Complete additional tasks – Ask teacher for help
Consequences of not having a corporate image/having a negative corporate image				
I understand the consequences of not having a corporate image/having a negative corporate image: • no recognisable brand • less professional reputation • staff are less consistent, so customers are not dealt with fairly				– Refer to instructions – Complete additional tasks – Ask teacher for help

8 Electronic communication

In this chapter you will learn about:

Method, features, uses and benefits of:

- blogs
- e-diary
- e-mail
- podcasts/vodcasts
- presentations
- social media
- video and audio conferencing
- websites

Blogs

Blogs are set up on the internet by individuals who wish to communicate their thoughts and opinions on a particular topic. There are blogs on virtually anything you can think of — photography, business, education, recipes, personal diaries, hobbies etc. Blogs can bring people from around the world who share similar interests together to share ideas, make friends and even do business together.

Electronic diaries

An electronic diary is held on a computer. While it includes many features of a paper-based diary, such as storing appointments, personal details, to-do list etc, it has many other features and advantages.

Advantages of a diary

- Recurring entries, for example weekly sales meetings, need only be printed once. This saves time writing for having to write the same information over and over.

- Alerts can be used to remind the user about an appointment.

- The diaries of several people may be linked and can be checked to find a suitable date/time for a meeting.

8 Electronic communication

In this chapter you will learn about:

Methods, features, uses and benefits of:

- blogs
- e-diary
- e-mail
- podcasts/vodcasts
- presentations
- social media
- video and audio conferencing
- webinars
- websites

Blogs

Blogs are set up on the Internet by individuals who wish to communicate their thoughts and opinions on a particular topic; there are blogs on virtually anything you can think of – photography, business, education, recipes, personal diaries, hobbies etc Blogs can bring people from around the world who share similar interests together to share ideas, make friends and even do business together.

Electronic diary (e-diary)

An electronic diary is held on a computer. While it includes many features of a paper-based diary, such as storing appointments, personal details, to-do lists etc, it has many other features and advantages.

Advantages of e-diary

- Recurring meetings, for example weekly sales meetings, need only be entered once. This saves time writing (or keying in) the same information over and over.

- Alerts can be used to remind the user about an appointment.

- The diaries of several people may be linked and can be checked to find a suitable date/time for a meeting.

- Double-booking of appointments is highlighted, bringing this to the attention of the user.

- Some electronic diaries will link to an e-mail facility and any changes made to appointments will be e-mailed to relevant people.

Electronic mail (e-mail)

E-mail is information sent and received via computer. Text, graphics and files can all be sent instantly from one computer to another (if both users have an e-mail address).

Uses and advantages of e-mail

- A fast method of sending (urgent) information. Messages can be sent instantly to anywhere in the world.

- A relatively inexpensive method of communication. It is cheaper than making a telephone call or posting a letter. E-mail can be sent, received, read and then deleted without using any paper, making it environmentally friendly and more relevant as many offices are now choosing to go paperless.

- Attachments can be sent easily. Previously prepared files such as spreadsheets, database files, letters or pictures can be attached to the e-mail. This means that the person receiving the attachment has the option to print, edit and/ or save the attached file to their computer. Sending a bulky document by e-mail is considerably cheaper than sending by post or courier.

- Group e-mail can be used. One e-mail can be prepared and sent to a number of different recipients at the same time. This ensures all recipients are sent the same information at the same time. Contact groups or distribution lists can be set up to include different people for different purposes.

- Messages can be flagged according to priority (high, low). This allows the recipient to prioritise the order in which he/she opens e-mail messages.

- A receipt/confirmation facility asks the recipient to let the sender know that they have received and opened the e-mail message they sent.

- Messages can be forwarded to other users. If someone receives a message they wish to let others see they can easily forward the e-mail to them.

- Copies (Cc) and blind copies (Bcc) of the e-mail can be sent to a number of people. If a Bcc is used, the initial recipient will be unaware that Bcc-ed person has also received the e-mail.

- E-mail is convenient and allows communication at any time of the day. This is very useful for sending messages across different time zones. For example if an organisation wishes to communicate with an overseas branch, the e-mail can be prepared and sent during the working day in one time zone and can be received and dealt with during the working day in another.

- Confidential information can be sent via e-mail as a password is usually required to access the e-mail accounts.

- Mailing lists can be created. Subscribers to a mailing list will receive e-mails containing relevant information on a regular basis – many businesses use this to send e-newsletters, announce any promotions etc.

Podcasts and vodcasts

A podcast/vodcast is an audio/video file that can be downloaded to a computer or mobile device (such as a smartphone or tablet). It means that people can listen or watch at a time that is convenient to them.

Presentation

Presentation software can be used to prepare slides that contain text, graphics, sound, animation etc. This is usually used when passing on information to an audience (see chapter 12 for more details).

Social media

Social media is a way of talking to other people via your computer, allowing you to exchange pictures, information, ideas, opinions etc. Social media is becoming more popular with businesses as a way to communicate with customers and potential customers.

- Twitter is an information network that connects people to the latest stories, ideas, opinions and news. Individuals choose to 'follow' whoever interests them, whether this is an individual, business, news outlet etc. Businesses can use Twitter to quickly share information about their products and services. It also allows a 'conversation' between the follower and the business about a product/service, which can then be 'retweeted' to many more potential customers.

- Facebook and Instagram are social networking services that let you connect with friends, co-workers, and others who share similar interests or who have common backgrounds. Businesses use these services as it gives them direct access to customers and potential customers.

- LinkedIn is a business version of Facebook – it connects individuals with people they know on a professional basis. It allows the user to see other people's business contacts and to ask for introductions in order to do business with them.

- Virtual learning environments (VLEs) use the Internet to allow remote access to learning materials, for example notes, tasks, homework, tests etc. Students can either work through the materials at their own pace before submitting to the 'teacher' for checking and tracking, or they can participate while a teacher conducts a live class – communicating through a microphone, chat rights, or by writing on the 'board'. Edmodo, Google Classroom and Microsoft Teams are examples of VLEs that you may have used in school.

Advantages of social media

- Individuals usually 'follow' or 'friend' organisations they are interested in. This allows an organisation to reach its target audience by providing information/special offers etc directly to potential customers, which could lead to increased sales.

- Many followers or friends will retweet or 'like' comments or posts. This helps an organisation to reach a wide audience because other individuals (who are not following the organisation) will see the comments or posts.

- Organisations now use social media as a marketing tool and as it is low cost/free to set up an account, this can help reduce costs. This raises awareness of the organisation.

- Customers can contact the organisation directly through social media. This increases customer engagement and if the organisation responds quickly and satisfactorily it can enhance the reputation of the organisation.

Video and audio conferencing (digital conferencing)

- Video conferencing allows people in different locations to hold face-to-face meetings. It is two-way, interactive communication meaning all parties taking part can display presentations and see the body language of people participating in the meeting. Mobile devices now make it even easier for face-to-face meetings to occur at convenient times of the day. Benefits of video conferencing include: cost savings (travel and accommodation), less time spent travelling (meaning more tasks can be carried out, leading to increased productivity) and the reduction of the organisation's carbon footprint (because travel is reduced).

- Audio conferencing has the same benefits of video conferencing – the main difference being that you cannot see the other people in the meeting – you can only hear them. Audio conferencing is becoming less popular due to the personal, face-to-face interaction that can be achieved with video conferencing.

Webinar

A webinar is a live presentation that uses the Internet to connect the individual hosting the webinar to an audience – members of the audience can be in any part of the world. Presenters can be seen by the audience speaking, using their computer screens for slideshows or demonstrations etc. The host can also invite guests from other locations to co-host the webinar with them.

Interactive features allow the audience to ask questions and chat with the host. Many people who host webinars include question and answer sessions at the end of the presentation to answer questions from the audience.

Websites

Many organisations will have their own website. They will use this to communicate with customers and potential customers – promoting their products with pictures, product details (size, colour etc) and customer reviews – to encourage people to buy the product or service. Many organisations have an e-commerce facility on their website, which allows customers to purchase products online.

Method

When communicating with customers, clients and employees it is important that the correct method of communication is used:

- Is it appropriate? Will all intended recipients receive the information?
- Is it the most cost effective?
- How quickly is the information required?

This table shows the ways that business organisations and charities use different methods of electronic communication.

Method of communication	Organisation	Charity
E-mail	• To contact customers about special offers. • To communicate with colleagues in different areas of the organisation. • To communicate with suppliers.	• To contact participants about upcoming events. • To contact organisations to request donations/sponsorship.
Text	• To send a reminder to staff about an upcoming meeting. • To contact managers urgently regarding problems/queries.	• To send a reminder to participants about the starting time of events.
Website	• To advertise products/services. • To allow online purchase of products (e-commerce). • To give background details on the organisation.	• To advertise the charity's fundraising activities and allow online registration. • To give background details on the charity. • To allow donations to be made online.
Blog	• To provide regular updates of events. • To allow the organisation to communicate with a wide audience. • To allow customers to interact with the organisation.	• To provide regular updates of events, amounts raised etc • To show photographs and videos of previous events.

(continued)

Method of communication	Organisation	Charity
Podcast	• To allow a wide audience to listen to interviews with senior managers.	• To allow a wide audience to listen to success stories about the charity. • To allow people to listen to interviews with participants of events.
Video/audio conferencing	• To allow managers to hold meetings with employees in different locations.	• To allow planning of events.
Social media	• To interact with customers or potential customers, for example through special offers.	• To promote charitable events.
Webinar	• To hold training sessions with employees.	• To give presentations on how people have benefitted from the charity. • To give presentations on future events and preparations required, for example climbing Kilimanjaro.

⚠ Watch point

Always read all questions carefully and ensure your answer is relevant to the question. In the 2017 Assignment, candidates were asked to give the advantages to a charity of using social media, so they needed to ensure their answer was directly related to a **charity** and not just simply a business organisation.

❓ Theory questions

1. Describe **three** advantages of using e-mail.
2. Describe **three** advantages of using an electronic diary.
3. Outline the following methods of electronic communication:
   (a) podcast
   (b) video conferencing
   (c) webinar
4. Explain a business use of each of the following:
   (a) social media
   (b) video conferencing
   (c) website
5. Complete the following table with the most appropriate method of electronic communication.

Information	Appropriate method of electronic communication
Announcement of special offers to customers/potential customers	
Information on products – details, pictures etc	
Information to all employees working in the Sales Department	
Meeting scheduled for next week with all heads of departments	
Feedback from customers	

Skill

- Decision-making
- ICT
- Research
- Literacy
- Employability
- Skills for learning, life and work

Exam practice

1. Download the file *Electronic Communication EP1* from the Leckie and Leckie website.

   (a) Complete the task.

   (b) Insert your own name as a footer and print one copy of the completed task.

2. Download the file *Electronic Communication EP2* from the Leckie and Leckie website.

   (a) Complete the task.

   (b) Insert your own name as a footer and print one copy of the completed task.

Learning Checklist

Skills, knowledge and understanding	Strength ☺	☺	Weakness ☹	Next steps
Methods, features, uses and benefits of electronic communication				
I understand the methods, features, uses and benefits of electronic communication: • blog • e-diary • e-mail • podcasts/vodcasts • presentation • social media • video and audio conferencing • webinar • website				– Refer to instructions – Complete additional tasks – Ask teacher for help

2

IT Applications

9 Word-processing/Desktop publishing

In this chapter you will learn about

- Formatting functions required in word-processing and desktop publishing.
- Business documents you may be asked to prepare.

What should I be able to do?

An administrator will support the work of the organisation by providing word-processing support. This includes keying in (preparing), editing and updating a variety of documents.

Any documents that are word processed by the administrator must be accurate and contain no spelling or grammatical errors. It could harm the reputation of an efficient organisation if documents are sent to customers that are not presented to a professional standard. It is therefore very important that the administrator takes time to check over the work – this is known as proofreading. While the spell check and grammar check functions of the software are very useful and should be used, they should never be used as an alternative to proofreading all documents.

House style

In order that all documents that originate from the same organisation look similar, a house style is used. This ensures that all staff use the same layouts when completing documents. There may be a house style book that staff can refer to, or documents may be stored as templates on the organisation's Intranet for staff to access. The use of house style documents will enhance the organisation's corporate image.

Formatting

Text formatting

To emphasise a relevant section of work or perhaps when preparing headed paper or a notice, you may be required to change how the text looks. Text formatting can include:

⚠ Watch point

Word-processing is a skill. It can take time to develop this skill. Practice is very important.

⚠ Watch point

It is important to maintain a professional image when preparing documents to communicate information. This could enhance the organisation's corporate image.

⚠ Watch point

Whatever house style you use you **must** ensure consistency within a document. For example, dates and times must follow the same format throughout the whole of the document.

⚠ Watch point

If you are asked to increase or decrease the size of font, ensure that you make it obvious you have done so, for example increase the font from 10 pt to 18 pt.

Change of size (unless this is also specifically asked for in the question)	<u>Underline</u>	**Bold**
Italics	Shading	Colour (only accepted when printed in colour)
Font change (unless this is also specifically asked for in the question)	Right alignment	Centre
Justification	Borders	• Bullet points
WordArt	Text within a shape	

Page formatting

Page formatting includes changing margins, changing the orientation (portrait/landscape) and changing the page size (such as creating an A5 booklet).

Using templates

The use of templates will save time in the design stage of producing a document. Most word-processing and desktop publishing packages will have a range of templates that can be used. For example:

Advertisements   Award Certificates   Banners   Business Forms   Catalogues

The user can select the template of their choice and then simply edit the text/graphics. Templates can be customised by inserting company logos, addresses and other items in the appropriate places.

Set and change margins and line spacing

A default margin is set when you open a new document. You may be instructed to change the default. Line spacing can be single, 1.5 or double. You may be asked to select the whole document to change the line spacing, or to only change selected text, for example one paragraph. You must highlight the text to be changed before performing the line spacing function.

⚠ Watch point

Always consider how your finished document will look – too many examples of text formatting in one document can be distracting and will not enhance your document.

⚠ Watch point

Margins are shown on the left/right and top/bottom of the document. Ensure that you read instructions carefully and change the appropriate margins.

Insert, delete and move text/cut and/or copy and paste
You may be asked to insert additional text. If doing this you must ensure that all line spacing remains consistent. Text may be deleted by highlighting it and pressing the **backspace** or **delete** key. To move text, the **cut and paste** function can be used – always double check that all text to be moved has been selected before selecting 'cut'. The spacing between paragraphs should always be checked once a cut and paste is completed.

Find and replace text
You may be asked to identify a specific word within the document that should be consistently replaced by another word. Always proofread your work to ensure all required words have been changed.

Carry-out manuscript corrections
Once a document has been printed it should be given a final check. If any changes are to be made to the printed document they should be made using manuscript correction signs.

Manuscript correction signs

Margin sign	Text sign	Meaning
l.c.	conFerence	Lower case letter
NP	[The long winding...	New paragraph
run on	...at last. / Then the traffic...	No new paragraph – carry straight on
stet	~~regardless~~	Do not delete – the word with a broken line underneath should be included.
u/l	The newest recruit	Underline text
trs	white and black	Transpose words (or characters). This means change the order of the words/characters.
CAPS	School	Capital letters
u.c.	john Smith	Capital or upper case letter
close up	Edin burgh	Remove space
del	The ugly duckling	Delete letter or word
ʌquick	The brown fox	Insert letter or word
black		Make word clearer
⊙	The end of the sentence ʌ	Insert a full stop

Enhance text, eg apply bold, italics and underline

These formats can be used to make relevant or important text more obvious or to enhance the overall document. Ensure that these enhancements are used thoughtfully and consider how the finished document will look – is the **relevant** *information* <u>obvious</u>?

Align text

The default for text is left aligned – this means all text starts at the same point on the left-hand side of the page. However, text can also be centred in the middle of the document, right aligned (all text starts at the right hand side of the page) or justified (all text starts at the same point and ends at the same point – like in the pages of this book)!

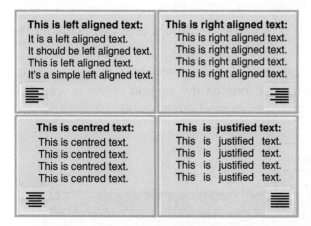

Insert graphics

Graphics can be used to enhance your document. However, always make sure that any graphic is relevant to the content of the document. Ensure that all of the graphic is visible – that it is not clipped. Also, graphics should not cover any text.

Use bullets and numbering

It is common for brief points in a list to be bulleted or numbered. It draws the attention of the reader to important information. Different styles of bullets are available – choose which one you prefer and stick to it, this ensures consistency within the document.

- These are some of the styles of bullets you can use.
○ These are some of the styles of bullets you can use.
✓ These are some of the styles of bullets you can use.
➢ These are some of the styles of bullets you can use.
❖ These are some of the styles of bullets you can use.

Insert headers and footers, both manual and custom

Headers and footers are used to display additional information, for example chapter headings or a slogan.

⚠ **Watch point**

Punctuation should not be enhanced in any way – always check when using bold/italics/underline etc at the end of a sentence that you have not enhanced the full stop – this is a common error!

⚠ **Watch point**

If you are required to include a header or footer you must ensure no other information (such as your name, school etc) is on the same line as the information requested in the task. Personal details must **always** appear underneath any other header or footer information.

⚠ **Watch point**

When using shading, ensure that all text can still be clearly seen.

⚠ **Watch point**

You may be asked to only include page numbers on certain pages of your document. Ensure you know how to do this.

Borders and shading

Borders and shading are another method of emphasising text within a document. Borders can be placed around certain information in the document or around the whole page.

Page numbering

If a document has a few pages it may be a good idea to number them so that if they get mixed up it is easy for the reader to identify which page comes next. Page numbers have many different styles and can be placed in the header or footer. It is common practice **not** to include page numbers on a cover/title page.

Creating and enhancing tables

Tables can be used to present information more clearly for the user.

You may have a word-processing checklist that you use to evaluate your progress through this section of the course. This will probably have been created using a table.

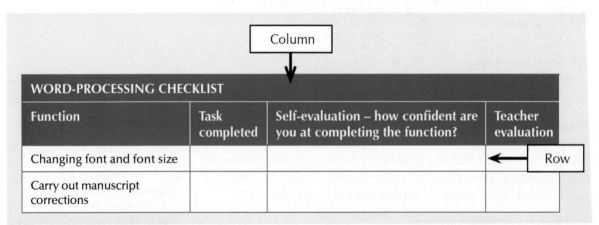

WORD-PROCESSING CHECKLIST			
Function	Task completed	Self-evaluation – how confident are you at completing the function?	Teacher evaluation
Changing font and font size			
Carry out manuscript corrections			

Add or delete row(s) and column(s)

Rows can be added easily at the bottom of the table. However, read all instructions carefully and if the row has to be inserted into the middle of the table, ensure you follow the instructions for your software. To delete a row in a table, highlight the row and follow the instructions specific to your software – ensure lines in the table are also deleted.

Columns can be inserted at any point in the table. They can also be deleted if they are no longer required. Follow instructions specific to your software to do this.

Borders and shading

When a table is displayed, borders are shown around each 'cell' (or box). These can be removed – either around the whole table or around specific boxes.

Shading can be used to emphasise information contained within the table. In the example shown below the total amount due has been shaded.

Sort data on one or two columns

Information within the table can be displayed in a specific order required by the user. The table can be sorted in ascending or descending order on one or two columns.

Merge cells and alignment of data

Information can be displayed over two columns or rows using the merge facility. Text can also be shown at different angles within a cell, i.e. rotated, and left/centre/right aligned within a cell.

Formulae

You can perform calculations within a table – this is useful if the information is contained in your word-processed document and not in a spreadsheet. Simple calculations such as SUM can be calculated in a table.

Example of a table that has been formatted.

> **⚠ Watch point**
>
> Ascending = A–Z (going up).
> Descending = Z–A (going down).

Order Form				
To	EVA GAMES Ltd 27 Glen Road INVERNESS IV6 7YH			
REF NO	QUANTITY	DESCRIPTION	UNIT PRICE	TOTAL PRICE
EG125	4	Connect 4	£5.99	£24.95
EG352	10	Snakes and Ladders	£3.99	£39.99
		TOTAL AMOUNT DUE		£59.94

Order Form has been merged and centred over five columns.

Borders have been removed from this section as these columns are not required.

This text is wrapped to ensure it fits into one cell

The table has been sorted in ascending order of total price.

Shading has been used to highlight the total amount due – an important figure!

The formula function has been used to calculate the total amount due.

Importing data from IT applications into a document

You may be asked to insert information from a spreadsheet, database or word-processing package into a document. You must ensure all information is placed in the correct position (you may need to read the wording within the document) and that all information is visible and clear to the reader.

Merging appropriate data from spreadsheet and database applications into a business document

The merge function can be used to personalise business documents. Information from database tables and spreadsheets previously created can be merged with a word-processed document to personalise letters, name badges, certificates etc.

Printing documents and extracts of documents

You should be able to print the completed document, specific pages of the document and documents showing merge fields.

Standard formats for date and time

When keying in the date, the following formats are acceptable:

3 June 2018	03 June 2018	3rd June 2018	June 3rd 2018
3/6/18	03/06/18	June 3, 2018	Sunday, 03 June 2018

All dates must include the year.
The following would not be acceptable:

the 3rd of June 2018	3rd of June 2018	American dates in number format eg 6/20/18

A variety of formats is also acceptable when keying in the time:

1100 hours	1100 hrs	11:00 hours	11.00 hrs
11 am	11 am	11.00 am	11.00 am

Full stops should not be used when keying 'am' or 'pm' in the time. The following would not be acceptable:

11.00 a.m	1 p.m.

⚠ Watch point

Consistency is key! If using an e-file that includes a date and/or time you must ensure you follow the same style as used previously. **Never change styles within a task.**

GO! Practice task 1

The following document has been checked for errors after being printed.

> **ADMINISTRATIVE ASSISTANT** *Increase size*
>
> *uc*
> *trs*
> *uc*
> *close up*
>
> An Administrative assistant has many duties and tasks to fulfil within an organisation. He/she is responsible for supporting the organisation by sending and receiving e-mails, photocopying, answering telephone enquiries, organising events etc. skills required by an Administrative Assistant include communication skills, ICT skills as well as literacy and numeracy skills.
>
> *Bold*
> *bold \ Job*
>
> When applying for a job as an Administrative Assistant it is important you look at the Job Description and Person Specification to find out if you would have all the skills, qualities and qualifications required by the organisation. A Description will also detail the tasks and duties required to be undertaken as part of the job. The Job Description is a useful document as it will help you decide if you would like to carry out the duties/tasks associated with the role. Both documents will give you a good idea if you would be suitable for the position.
>
> *Run on*
>
> These documents should be included in the recruitment pack you will receive when applying for the job.

Download the file WPDTPPT1 from the Leckie and Leckie website.

1. Make the changes shown above.
2. Insert your own name as a footer and print one copy of the completed task.

GO! Practice task 2

Download the file WPDTPPT2 from the Leckie & Leckie website and make the amendments shown below.

1. Change the font and increase the size of the main heading.
2. Change the margins to 4 cm/1.58".
3. Embolden all shoulder headings.
4. Insert the following text as a third paragraph in the 'Iron deficiency' section:

   In contrast, tannins found in tea reduce the absorption of iron, so it's better to have a glass of orange juice with your breakfast cereal rather than a cup of tea.

5. Move the section (including the heading) headed 'Vegetarianism' to below the section 'Calcium Deficiency'.
6. In the 'Foods to Choose' section, italicise all the recommendations for teenagers – starting from 'Plenty of starchy carbohydrates' and ending with 'Take regular exercise'.
7. Embolden and underline the section on acne.
8. Bullet point all information in the 'Key Points' section.
9. Insert an appropriate graphic.
10. Justify the document.
11. Insert your name and school in a header.
12. Insert the page numbers in the footer and right align them.
13. Print one copy of the document.

GO! Practice task 3

Your school's Christmas music concert will take place on the second Friday in December at 7 pm. Tickets will cost £5 for adults and £3 for children and concessions.

Create the following items for the concert:

1. Tickets
2. A poster
3. Invitations to be sent to local councillors

⚠ Watch point

In Newsletter tasks a presentation mark is normally given – the marker will check that the candidate has made full use of the page and the Newsletter is aesthetically pleasing. Remember to include the word 'Newsletter' as well as the date.

★ Exam practice

1. Borders Community Group is to host a Book Fayre in Hawick Town Hall. You have been asked to complete a letter. Download the file *WPDTP EP1* from the Leckie & Leckie website.

   (a) Insert a suitable reference and date.

   (b) Action and delete the comments within the file.

   (c) Include the following as the third paragraph:

   We are always keen to use the Town Hall for the benefit of our local community. If you have any ideas for events that you feel may encourage community spirit please contact me on 01450567149.

   (d) Insert another row in the table and insert the following information (at the appropriate point):

   Mhairi Greenhorn. 11.45 am. Writing masterclass.

   (e) Send a copy of this standard letter to all people who expressed an interest in community events – the list can be found in the database file *WPDTP EP1* (download from the Leckie and Leckie website). Print one copy of the letter showing the merge fields and a copy of one merged letter.

2. Download the file *WPDTP EP2* from the Leckie and Leckie website.

   (a) Create and print a newsletter. Ensure suitable graphics, a logo and formatting are used. The newsletter must fit onto one page.

   (b) Print one copy of the newsletter.

3. Download the file *WPDTP EP3* from the Leckie and Leckie website.

   (a) Complete the task.

   (b) Print one copy of the completed order form.

🌳 Skill

- ICT skills
- Literacy
- Numeracy
- Employability
- Skills for learning, life and work

Learning Checklist

Skills, knowledge and understanding	Strength ☺		Weakness ☹	Next steps
Creating and editing a range of documents in line with house style. The documents may contain multiple pages				
I can create and edit a range of documents in line with house style. The documents may contain multiple pages: • letters (such as application, thank you and enquiry) • business reports • forms (such as travel and booking forms) • minutes • agendas • itineraries • posters • booklets • newsletters • name badges/business cards/compliments slips/wristbands				– Refer to instructions – Complete additional tasks – Ask teacher for help
Using a variety of word-processing and desktop publishing skills				
I can use a variety of word-processing and desktop publishing skills: • text formatting • page formatting • using templates • select and/or change font and font size • set and change margins and line spacing • insert, delete and move text • find and replace text • cut and/or copy and paste • carry out manuscript corrections • enhance text, eg bold, italics and underline • align text • insert graphics • bullets and numbering • insert headers and footers, both manual and custom • borders and shading • page numbering				– Refer to instructions – Complete additional tasks – Ask teacher for help

(continued)

Creating and enhancing a table

I can create and enhance a table: • insert, delete or amend data • add or delete row(s) and column(s) • borders and shading • merge cells • alignment of data, eg centre within cell, text direction • formulae (sum only) • sort data on one or two columns				– Refer to instructions – Complete additional tasks – Ask teacher for help

Importing data from IT applications into a document

I can import data from IT applications into a document: • data and/or chart from a spreadsheet file • data from a database file • data from a word-processing/DTP file • information from the Internet				– Refer to instructions – Complete additional tasks – Ask teacher for help

Merging appropriate data from spreadsheet and database applications into a business document

I can merge appropriate data from spreadsheet and database applications into a business document: • labels • letters • reports • name badges • forms • certificates				– Refer to instructions – Complete additional tasks – Ask teacher for help

Using comments

I can use comments: • add • action • delete				– Refer to instructions – Complete additional tasks – Ask teacher for help

Printing documents and extracts of documents

I can print documents and extracts of documents: • completed document in different layouts (such as A4 and A5) • documents showing merge fields • specific pages				– Refer to instructions – Complete additional tasks – Ask teacher for help

10 Databases

What is a database?

A database is a collection of related information. A database allows us to search for information very quickly and to sort the information easily. The required data may then be presented in the form of a printed report.

Flat database

A **flat database** contains one file or table of data.

- Each file is made up of a collection of records.
- A record is the information about one person/thing (a collection of fields).
- A field is a single piece of information about the person/thing.

For example, one record – for Melissa Hughes – contains seven fields.

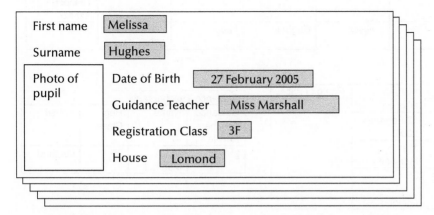

| First name | Melissa |
| Surname | Hughes |

Photo of pupil

Date of Birth   27 February 2005

Guidance Teacher   Miss Marshall

Registration Class   3F

House   Lomond

In the database file above, the information about the Guidance Teacher is not specific to the one pupil; several pupils will have the same Guidance Teacher. This means that the Guidance Teacher information will be repeated through the records. There are obviously disadvantages to having data repeated:

- It takes a long time to enter the data.

- It takes up more memory storage in the computer.

- If the data has to be edited, this would have to be carried out for every record.

Relational database

A **relational database** can have more than one file or table of data. In the example shown, the same pupil record is displayed but the data is made up from two different tables. The two tables are linked through the Guidance Teacher Ref No field as this is shown in both tables. This will reduce the amount of data being repeated in the database. The Guidance Teacher Ref No field is known as the **primary key**. Each Guidance Teacher would be allocated a unique number that would identify them. The name of the teacher cannot be a primary key as more than one teacher might have the same name.

Pupil table					
Pupil Number	First Name	Surname	Photo	Date of Birth	Guidance Teacher Ref No
001	Melissa	Hughes	Image	27 February 2005	LMA1

First name	Melissa
Surname	Hughes
Date of Birth	27 February 2005
Guidance Teacher	Miss Marshall
Registration Class	3F
House	Lomond

Photo of pupil

Guidance Teacher table			
Guidance Teacher Ref No	Name	Reg Class	House
LMA1	Miss Marshall	3F	Lomond

Creating forms

A selection or all of the fields from one/both tables can be used to create a form. This allows records to be seen using a much easier layout/format. The field that appears in both tables (eg ID, Reference/Account Number) should only appear once. It is then simpler for the administrator to insert new records as all field entries can be made on one screen. It is important to check that all Field Names are visible, i.e. not truncated by the Field Entry boxes. If Field Names/Entry boxes need to be adjusted then this can be done in the **Design View.** A Form **Wizard** can be used to create forms.

- A form should always have an appropriate heading – this is usually entered in the form header and appears at the top of the form. Always use block capitals for form headings. Graphics/logos can also be inserted in the form header.

- A form footer can be used to display information at the end of the form.

- Page footers can be inserted to display information at the bottom of each page.

Creating reports

Reports are used to display data. They can be used to print out all the data in a database or to print selected fields/records generated from a query. Reports cannot be used for entering/ editing data – they are for displaying data. A **Report Wizard** can be used to create reports.

- A report should always have an appropriate heading – this is usually entered in the report header and appears at the top of the report. Always use block capitals for report headings. Graphics/logos can also be inserted in the form header.

⚠ Watch point

Your own name and task details must appear **below** any report/page footer.

- A report footer can be used to display information at the end of the report.

- Page headers/footers can be inserted to display information at the bottom of each page.

Using a **Report Wizard** will allow you to:

- Specify the table/query to be used.

- Choose the layout for the report, for example in columns.

- Specify the order of the fields, any groupings (to reduce the duplication of information).

- Change the page setup to landscape (to allow the report to fit on one page).

- Insert an appropriate heading.

⚠ Watch point

Always check that your completed report contains the same number of records as your query.

The database user can use the design view to carry out any additional editing/formatting to enhance the report, such as inserting graphics (company logos etc) and formatting text (font, size, colour, etc).

Creating labels

Labels can be created from the information contained in a table/query/search. These can be used for mailing purposes – sending documents to customers/suppliers using the postal system – or for producing name badges etc.

Mr Robert Milligan
RM Enterprises
422 Montrose Street
Stirling
FK4 7FM

New Business Event 2018

A **Labels Wizard** can be used to insert the appropriate fields into a label layout. (This layout can be changed as required.) When creating address labels, each part of the address should be inserted on a new line and names must include Title, First Name and Surname. If a company/organisation name is provided then this must also be included. Any additional text/headers/footers that must be added to the labels (such as the purpose of the address labels) can be inserted in the design layout.

⚠ Watch point

Labels can only be assessed in the Question Paper.

Editing a database – inputting and editing data

An administrator would usually carry out tasks that involve inputting data and editing a database rather than creating a database.

Inputting data can be done using forms or tables. Forms make it easier for the user to add and edit data as only one record is displayed on screen at a time. Most database software will have a wizard to help create a form. The user is able to customise the form by using the **design view**: logos can be inserted, fonts/sizes can be changed, footers can be added. A form footer will appear at the bottom of the form and a page footer will appear at the bottom of each page.

Editing a database – formatting

The field format describes the way the data is held. Fields can be formatted to display text, numbers, dates, currency, Yes/No or use a Lookup Wizard (used to store options for the user to select from when entering the data). Dates can be formatted in different ways, for example 8 December 2012 (long date), 08/12/12 (short date) or 08-Dec-12 (medium date). Numbers and currency can be formatted to show a specified number of decimal places.

Adding/deleting fields/records

You can add fields or delete fields by using the design view in a table/datasheet or a form. A field can be added or inserted into an appropriate place in the design view. It must be formatted appropriately – text, number, etc. You must return to the table or form to fill in the appropriate details for all records. A field can be deleted from the design view. However, once a field has been deleted **all** the contents will automatically be deleted.

Whether working in table or form view, you can easily add new records. There will be an appropriate button for you to click on to create a new blank record, and then the appropriate details must be keyed in. All new records will appear at the end of the database. A sort can be carried out to rearrange the records appropriately (see page 84). Any record can be selected and deleted (select the appropriate record, right click and choose delete), which will permanently remove it from the database, for example if an employee has left the organisation, their record must be deleted (under the GDPR, see Chapter 4, page 39).

Searching information in a relational database

Searching for data in a database can be carried out in different ways. It is possible to search the database for an exact match in one or more fields or to use different operators as shown below:

⚠ Watch point

Any data added to a database table/form must be consistent with what is already there.

⚠ Watch point

Any new fields inserted must be consistent with the existing fields – such as the capitalisation of field heading.

⚠ Watch point

A query will allow searching and sorting to be carried out at the same time.

Operator	Explanation	Example(s)
= (equals)	Simply by keying in the word to be found **or** by keying in = before the word to be found.	• To find all employees working in the Sales Department: you would enter the word *Sales* in the *Department* field. • To find all the customers who live in Glasgow with the surname Smith: you would enter the word *Glasgow* in the *Town* field and also enter the word *Smith* in the *Surname* field.
> (greater than)	Key in the greater than symbol (>) before a number/ date.	• To find all Sales Representatives who have sold goods of more than £10,000: you would enter *>10000* (the field should have been formatted as currency and therefore you do not enter the £ or ,) in the *Total Sales* field. • To find all employees who were born after 31 December 1980: you would enter *>31/12/1980* in the *Date of Birth* field.
>= (greater than or equal to)	Key in the greater than symbol (>) followed by the equals symbol (=) before a number/ date.	• To find all Sales Representatives who have sold goods of £10,000 or more: you would enter *>=10000* (the field should have been formatted as currency and therefore you do not enter the £ or ,) in the *Total Sales* field. • To find all employees who were born on or after 31 December 1980: you would enter *>=31/12/1980* in the *Date of Birth* field.
< (less than)	Key in the less than symbol (<).	• To find all Sales Representatives who have sold goods of less than £10,000: you would enter *<10000* (the field should have been formatted as currency and therefore you do not enter the £ or ,) in the *Total Sales* field. • To find all employees who were born before 31 December 1980: you would enter *<31/12/1980* in the *Date of Birth* field.
<= (less than or equal to)	Key in the less than symbol (<) followed by the equals symbol (=) before a number/ date.	• To find all Sales Representatives who have sold goods of £10,000 or less: you would enter *<=10000* (the field should have been formatted as currency and therefore you do not enter the £ or ,) in the *Total Sales* field. • To find all employees who were born on or before 31 December 1980: you would enter*<=31/12/1980* in the *Date of Birth* field.
Or	Key in the first word to be found then the word OR followed by the second word to be found.	• To find all the customers who live in Glasgow or Edinburgh: you would enter *Glasgow OR Edinburgh* in the *Town* field. • To find all the customers who live in Glasgow or Edinburgh with the surname Smith: you would enter *Glasgow OR Edinburgh* in the *Town* field **and** also enter the word *Smith* in the *Surname* field.
Not	Key in the word NOT followed by the word not to be included in the results.	• To find all the customers who do not live in Dumfries: you would enter *NOT Dumfries* in the *Town* field.
Is null	Key in the words IS NULL	• To find the names of pupils who have not yet provided their passport number you would enter IS NULL in the passport number field to find any records where this information has not been inserted.

A query can be created to carry out searching tasks, which allows the results to be saved.

Searching for data in a database can be carried out on only one field, which is called a **simple** search; or on more than one field, which is called a **complex** search.

Sorting information in a relational database

Sorting data in a database can be carried out in different ways:

- **Alphabetical** – data can be sorted on a field (which has been formatted as text) to be shown in alphabetical order, for example by surname.

- **Numerical** – data can be sorted on a field (which has been formatted as number) to be shown in numerical order, for example by account number.

- **Chronological** – data can be sorted on a field (which has been formatted as date/time) to be shown in chronological (date/time) order, for example by date of birth.

Data can be sorted in any one of these ways into ascending or descending order.

A query can be created to carry out sorting tasks, which allows the results to be saved.

Sometimes it may be necessary to carry out a sort using more than one field. This is known as a **complex** sort. For example, if the data is to be organised into alphabetical order by surname, the database may contain more than one person with the same surname. It is possible to carry out a sort that will organise the surname field into alphabetical order first and then organise the first name field into alphabetical order next. For example:

Surname	First Name
Smith	Alan
Smith	Grace
Smith	Henry
Smith	Sarah
Smith	Thomas

However, it would be normal practice to have these two fields shown in the order First Name, Surname. Make sure you understand how your school's software does this.

Printing

When printing data from a database it is important that all the required information is visible. If it is not, then you must go to the **design view** and adjust the appropriate field lengths so that the entries can be seen in full. Printing can be done as:

- table

- query – showing the results of a search/sort, selected records/fields

- form – you may be asked to print only one form

- report – effectively displaying the table/query

- labels – you may be asked to print only one page of labels

GO! Practice task 1

Download the folder *Databases PT1* from the Leckie and Leckie website.
You work for a local book club. Complete the following tasks.

1. Add a new field to the Reps table – E-mail Address. Insert the following information:

Mr Christopher Marshall	c.marshall@yahaa.co.uk
Mr David Hayes	dhayes4@mailit.com
Ms Gemma Tyler	gemmagirl@yahaa.co.uk
Miss Hazel Montague	hazmon@yahaa.co.uk
Mr Kevin Hughes	mrhughes14@eol.com
Mr Peter Murphy	murphypeter@eol.com
Mr Marco Hof	thehof@eol.com
Ms Liz Roberts	lizzie100@yahaa.co.uk

Print a copy of the Reps table in alphabetical order of book type and surname.

2. Create a form showing all the fields. Use the information below to update the database for a new customer (Rep No 1002):

Dr Kim Porter, 87b Portobello Drive, Dalkeith, EH13 2HR

Print a copy of the new form.

3. Information packs on new publications must be sent to each of the customers who order Children's Fiction books. Prepare address labels for these customers. Sort in alphabetical order of surname and include 'Children's Fiction' at the bottom of every label.

Print a copy of the labels.

4. Search for the customers of Christopher Marshall living in Edinburgh.

Print the results as a report showing only the customers' contact details. Insert a suitable heading – the logo should be inserted at the top right-hand side.

Practice task 2

Download the folder *Databases PT2* from the Leckie and Leckie website.

Pupils at Arden High School will be taking part in the Scottish Schools Music Festival next month. The database file contains the details for the pupils who will be participating.

1. Add a new field to the Pupil table – Participated Before?:

   All pupils except the S1 pupils, Katie O'Malley (4D) and Colin Hewitson (6B) have participated before. Update the Pupil table.

2. Print a copy of the Pupil table showing all fields except Guidance Teacher. Sort the data: show those who have participated before first and in alphabetical order of surname.

3. Mr O'Malley has just provided information on another pupil who should be added to the list:

Stuart Wallace (3C)
Performed last year playing the saxophone
Consent Form still to be received

   Add this pupil to the database using a form. Insert a form footer 'Scottish schools Music Festival [this year]'.

   Print a copy of the new form.

4. Mr O'Malley needs a list of all his pupils who have not yet returned their Consent Forms.

   Print the results of this search showing only the pupil name and class.

5. Provide a report of the S4 pupils who play in the string section (violin and cello). Show only the pupil names and the instruments played. Sort into order of musical instrument and pupil name. Insert a suitable heading and the school logo at the top right-hand side.

★ Exam practice

1. Download the folder *Databases EP1* from the Leckie and Leckie website.

   You work for *Walking Scotland*, a family-run business that specialises in organising walking holidays. The business is preparing for next month's walks.

   The database file *Databases EP1* contains the details of the walkers.

   (a) (i) Change the format of the DOB field to long date.

      Print the Walkers table showing the walkers' names, dates of birth and e-mail addresses in alphabetical order of surname.

(ii) Update the database: Mr James Ward has retired and has now been replaced by Mr Campbell Struthers who will be the Guide for the same route. His mobile number is 07321873346.

Print the Guides table showing the guides' names, walking routes and mobile numbers.

(b) Another walker has signed up for The West Highland Way. Her name is Siobhan Williams, DOB 8/4/82. Her e-mail address is williamss@eul.com. Update the database to include this information.

Create a form showing **all** the fields from the Walkers table except the e-mail address, plus the guide name and walking route from the Guides table. Insert a form header – Walk Information

Print a copy of Siobhan's form.

(c) Labels need to be created to be attached to each walker's map pack. This label should show their name and the walking route. Insert next month and the current year at the bottom of every label. Sort in order of walking route and walker's surname.

Print only the first page of the labels.

(d) Search for a list of all walkers born before 1990, except those walking The Three Lochs Way. These walkers will be invited to take part in a series of interviews with *Scottish Walking* magazine to feature in an upcoming publication.

Print the results as a report showing only the name of the walker and the walking route. Sort in alphabetical order of walking route and walker's surname.

Insert a suitable heading – the *Walking Scotland* logo should appear at the top right-hand side.

2. Download the folder *Databases EP2* from the Leckie and Leckie website.

The Scottish Games is an annual field and track event being held in July. You will be working as an administrator to help organise and support the event this year.

(a) Events have now been allocated an appropriate field/track. Add a new field to the Participants Table – Field/Track No. Insert the information shown in the table on the next page.

Print a copy of the updated Participants table on one page.

(continued)

Field 1	Field 2	Track 1	Track 2
Tyne Athletics	Irvine Athletics	Doon Runners	Team Teviot
Arran	Team Afton	Lomond Harriers	Bannock Runners
Team Tummel	Team Esk	Leven Runners	Blackhill Harriers
Leith Harriers	Don Athletics	Rob's Runners	Team Nevis
Caledonian Athletics	Forth Athletics		
Clyde Athletics	Fruin		

(b) The coach, James Stewart, has asked for a list of all his teams participating on the Sunday. He would like this information to be printed as a table, sorted by team name, showing only the Team Name, Event and Field/Track No.

(c) Create a form and use the information below to update the database:

Coach 228 has advised of another team that will be participating and this has been confirmed – Glenan Runners will be competing in the Track event on the Saturday. There will be six participants in the team. The team will participate on Track 1.

Print a copy of the form for Glenan Runners.

(d) Clyde Athletics and Leith Harriers have now confirmed that they will be attending. Update the database as appropriate.

Prepare and print a report showing all confirmed teams with five or more participants. Show the name of the team (in alphabetical order) and the name of the coach fields only, in that order. Insert a suitable heading and the Scottish Games logo.

(e) Letters need to be sent to the coaches whose teams have still to confirm they will be attending. Prepare address labels for these letters. Insert the text CONFIRMATION at the bottom of every label.

Skill

- Literacy
- Numeracy
- Employability
- Skills for learning, life and work

Learning Checklist

Skills, knowledge and understanding	Strength ☺		Weakness ☹	Next steps
Creating forms				
I can create a form using selected fields from one or both tables, or a search				– Refer to instructions – Complete additional tasks – Ask teacher for help
I can create a form with a header and/or footer using text and/or graphics				– Refer to instructions – Complete additional tasks – Ask teacher for help
Creating reports				
I can create a report using selected fields from one or both tables, or a search				– Refer to instructions – Complete additional tasks – Ask teacher for help
I can create a report with a header and/or footer using text and/or graphics				– Refer to instructions – Complete additional tasks – Ask teacher for help
Creating labels				
I can create a labels from a table or search				– Refer to instructions – Complete additional tasks – Ask teacher for help
I can create labels with a header and/or footer				– Refer to instructions – Complete additional tasks – Ask teacher for help

(continued)

Editing a relational database

I can edit a relational database by inputting and editing data in tables or making use of forms				– Refer to instructions – Complete additional tasks – Ask teacher for help
I can edit a relational database by altering date format and decimal places				– Refer to instructions – Complete additional tasks – Ask teacher for help
I can edit a relational database by adding and deleting field(s) and record(s)				– Refer to instructions – Complete additional tasks – Ask teacher for help

Searching information in a relational database using operators

I can search information in a relational database using: • equals • greater than (>) • less than (<) • greater than or equal to (>=) • less than or equal to (<=) • OR • NOT • IS NULL				– Refer to instructions – Complete additional tasks – Ask teacher for help

Sorting information in a relational database on one or two fields

I can sort information in a relational database on one or two fields				– Refer to instructions – Complete additional tasks – Ask teacher for help

Printing

I can print tables, search results, specified fields, forms, reports and labels to fit on one page				– Refer to instructions – Complete additional tasks – Ask teacher for help

11 Spreadsheets

In this chapter you will learn about:

- Creating, editing and formatting a workbook.
- Applying advanced functions and formulae to a workbook.
- Using comments.
- Creating a chart and labelling it independently, using data from adjacent and non-adjacent columns and rows.
- Giving charts meaningful labels.
- Printing worksheets and extracts of worksheets.
- Printing charts.

What should I be able to do?

This part of the course requires you to solve business problems and present the solution using a spreadsheet.

What is a spreadsheet?

- A spreadsheet is a computer program designed to display and process numbers.

- It is a grid that is made up of cells, identified by column letters and row numbers.

- Each cell can contain text, numbers or formulae (to carry out calculations).

For example:

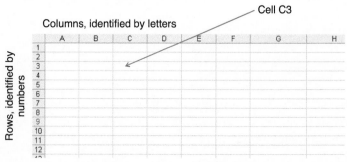

- A spreadsheet is a powerful tool for carrying out calculations and testing different mathematical possibilities.

- Simple calculations can be carried out, for example add (+), subtract (–), multiply (*) and divide (/).

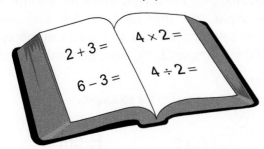

- More complex calculations can be carried out by using a range of built-in functions, for example add a range of cells (SUM), find the average (AVERAGE), find the highest number (MAX), etc.

You will learn more about calculations and functions later in this chapter.

Inserting and deleting rows/columns

By highlighting a column letter or row number, additional columns or rows can be inserted or selected ones can be deleted. Inserting columns/rows is useful if information has been omitted as it can be easily inserted into the correct position.

Hiding rows and columns

This is where rows and columns are temporarily removed from the spreadsheet (perhaps in order to see only some of the information). The information is not permanently deleted and can be seen again using the unhide command.

Formatting

Formatting means changing the way in which the information is displayed (for example, text alignment, borders and shading, font, size, style) or setting up a cell to contain numbers in a particular format (for example, £, %, date, decimal places).

Alignment of data
Text can be aligned horizontally, for example:

Left	Centre	Right

When using a spreadsheet package, text is automatically left aligned and numbers/values are automatically right aligned.

The direction of text within a cell can be rotated, for example:

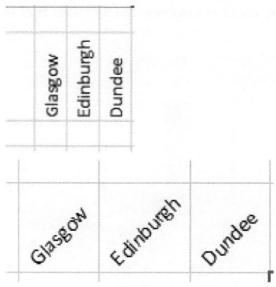

Or, text can be wrapped, to be shown over more than one line within a cell, and also aligned horizontally, for example:

This text is wrapped and left aligned	This text is wrapped and centre aligned	This text is wrapped and right aligned

Wrapping text is useful when inserting a long column heading.

Different fonts, styles, sizes
Cells can also be formatted for appearance, for example to show the contents as a specified size, in bold, underlined, or italicised.

Size	**Bold**	<u>Underline</u>	*Italics*

Formatting in this way helps identify information that is important, for example headings.

Formatting cells to currency, number and percentage to specified decimal places

A cell can be formatted to show any number entered to appear automatically with £, % or with a specified number of decimal places. For example:

Format number to show percentage	10%
Format number to show currency	£10.25
Format number to show specified number of decimal places, eg 2	7.50

Data format

You may be asked to insert the date using a particular format.

Formatted to short date	17/10/2018
Formatted to long date	17 October 2018
Custom format	17-Oct-18

Borders and shading

A cell can have a border or shading applied to make it stand out, for example:

This information stands out because of the border	This information stands out because of the shading

Applying advanced functions and formulae to a workbook

All formulae must start with '=' to tell the computer to carry out the calculation.

Basic arithmetic formulae

This type of formula uses only two cell references.

Arithmetic calculation → *Real-world example*	Arithmetic symbol/ function	Formula (explanation)
Add two numbers → *Calculate the total of two numbers*	+	=A1+A2 (contents of cell A1 added to contents of cell A2)
Subtract one number from another → *Calculate the difference between two numbers*	−	=A1−A2 (contents of cell A2 subtracted from contents of cell A1)
Multiply one number by another → *Calculate the total cost where you have cost per item and quantity*	*	=A1*A2 (contents of cell A1 multiplied by contents of cell A2)
Divide one number by another → *Calculate the percentage of items sold, for example the total of item 1 as a percentage of overall total sold*	/	=A1/A2 (contents of cell A1 divided by contents of cell A2)

When adding more than two cells you should use the SUM function (Σ).

Arithmetic calculation → *Real-world example*	Arithmetic symbol/function	Formula (explanation)
Add several numbers → *Calculate the total value of items sold when there are more than two items*	SUM	=SUM(A1:A10) (contents of the range of cells A1 through to A10 added together)

> ⚠ **Watch point**
>
> You must always use the most efficient method when inserting a formula. For example, even though you may achieve the correct answer with =A1+A2+A3+A4, this would not be awarded a mark in the exam because the most efficient way of doing this calculation would be to use the SUM function.

> ⚠ **Watch point**
>
> You should never use the word SUM in the same formula as +, −,÷ or ×. For example, do not use =Sum(A1+A2).

Functions: average, maximum, minimum, count, counta

Arithmetic calculation → *Real-world example*	Arithmetic symbol/function	Formula (explanation)
Calculate the average number → *Calculate the average cost from a list*	AVERAGE	=AVERAGE(A1:A10) (the average is calculated from the contents of the range of cells A1 through to A10)
Identify the highest number from a list → *Identify the best-selling product from a list*	MAX	=MAX(A1:A10) (the highest number is identified from the contents of the range of cells A1 through to A10)
Identify the lowest number from a list → *Identify the least popular product from a list*	MIN	=MIN(A1:A10) (the lowest number is identified from the contents of the range of cells A1 through to A10)
Count the number of entries in a list → *Count the number of products available for sale*	COUNT	=COUNT(A1:A10) (the number of cells containing a number is counted from the range of cells A1 through to A10)
Count cells that contain numbers/text/logical values/error values → *Count the number of deposits paid/not paid*	COUNTA	=COUNTA(A1:A10) (the number of cells containing a number/text/logical values/error values is counted from the range of cells A1 through to A10)

If (conditional formula)

Conditional formula – follow a course of action depending on the outcome (two possibilities)	IF	=IF(A1>50,10%,0) (if the contents of cell A1 are greater than 50 (true) then the value 10% will be entered, if the contents of cell A1 are not greater than 50 (false) then the value 0 will be entered)
A condition is set, followed by one outcome if true and an alternative outcome if false.		=IF(A1>50,'Yes','No') [two possible outcomes (yes or no), text must be inside inverted commas]
Calculate the value of discount given if 10% discount is allowed on orders over £50.		=IF(A1>50,A1*10%,0) (if the contents of cell A1 are greater than 50 (true) then the contents of cell A1 will be multiplied by 10% and this answer will be entered, if the contents of cell A1 are not greater than 50 (false) then the value 0 will be entered)

⚠ Watch point
You should never key in a formula containing functions, but use the function tool.

Linking cells within worksheets (working with multiple worksheets)
It is possible to refer to a cell in another worksheet in a formula or function. When a cell is linked the formula will not only show the cell reference but also the sheet name, for example, =A1*Sheet2!A3. (The contents of cell A1 in the current worksheet will be multiplied by the contents of cell A3 in the worksheet named Sheet 2.)

Using named cells
It can sometimes be difficult to understand a formula using cell references. It may be less confusing to give cells meaningful names. For example =A3*VAT.

Relative referencing
When the same calculation is to be repeated down a column/across a row, **replication** can be used to save time and reduce errors. This is a function of a spreadsheet package that allows the same calculation to be copied down/across without having to key in the formula/function again. The cell references will change relative to the new position. For example, replicating down will change the row numbers and replicating across will change the column letters.

⚠ Watch point
You should replicate formulae when repeating the same calculation, as this will save time and reduce errors.

```
=A1*B1
=A2*B2
=A3*B3
=A4*B4
=A5*B5
```

Absolute referencing

If a cell has been set up as an absolute reference in a formula (for example, A1) then this cell reference will not change during replication. The $ sign in front of the column and the $ sign in front of the row number tells the computer not to change it. To make a cell reference absolute the $ sign must appear in front of both the column letter and the row number. A named cell performs the same function as an absolute cell.

Comments

This is a feature in a spreadsheet package that can help you make a worksheet easier to understand by providing additional information about the data it contains. For example, you can use a **comment** as a note that provides information about data in an individual cell.

Or, a comment can be used to provide an instruction that must be carried out. If a comment has been added, a red triangle will appear at the top right corner, for example:

John	Brown
Adam	Lang
Patricia	Moffat
Angela	Carslaw

In order to read the comment you must move your cursor over the cell containing the comment and the instruction will appear, for example:

John	Brown	User:
Adam	Lang	Sort the surname into
Patricia	Moffat	alphabetical order
Angela	Carslaw	

Comments must be deleted once the instruction has been carried out.

Printing worksheets and extracts of worksheets

Spreadsheets can be printed:

- showing value view (figures)
- showing formulae view
- with or without gridlines
- with or without row and column headings
- in portrait or landscape orientation
- with headers and/or footers, both manual and custom
- to fit on one page

It is also possible to print only part of a spreadsheet (known as an **extract**).

If the full spreadsheet is not to be printed then it is possible to hide the column(s)/row(s) that are not to be shown on the printout. You must then **set the print area** before printing.

Creating a chart and labelling it independently

Data in a spreadsheet can be converted into graphical form, for example pie charts, bar charts and line graphs.

This makes the information easier to read and understand and it can be read at a glance.

Pie chart
This is used to show a **general comparison** where detail is not required. For example, to show the percentage of an organisation's spending by each department.

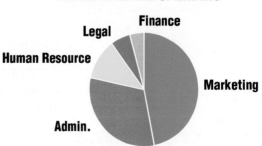

DEPARTMENTAL SPENDING

Bar (or column) chart
This is used to show **comparisons** over periods of time or between different products, for example, to compare the actual and target sales figures.

ACTUAL V TARGET SALES FIGURES

Line graph
This is used to show **trends** over a period of time. For example, to show how profits have risen or fallen over the last 6 months.

PROFIT IN LAST 6 MONTHS

Using data from adjacent and non-adjacent columns and rows
Information to be used in charts may be contained in cells that are side by side in the spreadsheet – these are known as adjacent cells and the cells can easily be highlighted to produce the required chart. However, it may be that the relevant information to be included in the chart is not contained in side-by-side cells – there may be a number of columns or rows between the required information. These are known as non-adjacent cells and you must select the correct cells. Your teacher will give you instructions for how to do this in the software that you are using.

In this example, you may be asked to create a chart for January Sales only. This would be using adjacent cells as you would use the information in cells A2 to B6 to create the chart.

	A	B	C	D	E
1	DEAKIN DESIGNS		SALES		
2	BRANCH	JANUARY	FEBRUARY	MARCH	TOTAL
3	Motherwell	£5,000	£4,500	£6,130	£15,630
4	Helensburgh	£4,000	£3,978	£4,002	£11,980
5	Falkirk	£2,500	£2,436	£2,690	£7,626
6	Dunfermline	£1,000	£908	£1,198	£3,106

In this example, you may be asked to create a chart for Total Sales. You would use the information contained in cells A2–A6 and E2–E6. These are non-adjacent cells.

	A	B	C	D	E
1	DEAKIN DESIGNS		SALES		
2	BRANCH	JANUARY	FEBRUARY	MARCH	TOTAL
3	Motherwell	£5,000	£4,500	£6,130	£15,630
4	Helensburgh	£4,000	£3,978	£4,002	£11,980
5	Falkirk	£2,500	£2,436	£2,690	£7,626
6	Dunfermline	£1,000	£908	£1,198	£3,106
7					

Giving charts meaningful labels

A spreadsheet package may have a charting function (chart wizard), which will allow the user to select the data to be included and then take the user step-by-step through the creation of the chart. Alternatively, the user may have to build the chart using specific menus/toolbar icons.

⚠ Watch point

You should know which is the *x*-axis and which is the *y*-axis.

- A chart will only be meaningful if it has been labelled appropriately.

- All charts should have a title that describes what the chart is displaying.

- Bar charts and line graphs must also have meaningful labels on the *x* and *y* axes.

- Data labels may also be used to identify the different segments of the chart.

- Legends help identify what the chart is actually displaying – include them as appropriate (they are not normally required if there is only a single bar/line or if data labels are included).

Points to note when creating a pie chart:

- The heading should include all relevant information (including the year, if appropriate). Use the wording from the question to help you decide what to include in the heading.

- It is good practice to put your heading in capitals – this will prevent you losing capitalisation marks.

- Ensure all segments are clearly identifiable when printed. Data labels can be helpful here. You will not be given marks if the segments cannot be identified.

- Check what data labels should be included (values, percentages, labels etc).

- Do not include a data label twice, i.e. in the chart and at the side or below the chart.

PERCENTAGE SALES FOR EACH BRANCH

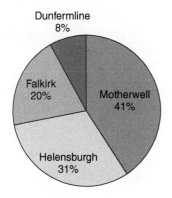

Printing charts

Charts can be printed as part of the spreadsheet or they can be printed as a separate sheet.

GO! **Practice task 1**

Download the file SSPT1 from the Leckie and Leckie website.
An organisation uses a spreadsheet to help keep track of the amount of money spent by each department each month.

(a) Open the spreadsheet file and use the information in it to complete the worksheet. Print one copy of the worksheet in value view with gridlines only, and one copy in formula view with gridlines and row and column headings.

(b) Create a bar chart to compare the spending of each department over the six-month period. Label the chart appropriately. Print the chart on a separate sheet.

(c) Create a pie chart to show the percentage of spending by each department. Include data labels and percentages as appropriate. Include an appropriate heading. Print the chart on a separate sheet.

Download the file *SS PT2* from the Leckie and Leckie website.

Hilltops Conference Centre is providing conference facilities for Ants Autos who are running a training session for all branch managers (on the first Tuesday of next month). Open the spreadsheet file and use the information in it and the e-mail below to complete both worksheets.

1. Print one copy of the **Price List** worksheet in value view with gridlines only, and one copy in formula view with gridlines, and row and column headings.

2. Print one copy of the **Invoice** worksheet in value view with gridlines only, and one copy in formula view with gridlines, and row and column headings.

To: Administrator

From: Antony

Date: Today's date

Subject: TRAINING SESSION

Hi

We require one main meeting room and two committee rooms for use throughout the day. We will also require hire of AV equipment. There will be 20 people attending the training session – they will all require tea and coffee, lunch and parking.

Regards

Antony

1. Download the file *SS EP1* from the Leckie and Leckie website.

   EK High School is running an excursion to Barcelona.

   (a) Open the spreadsheet file and use the information in it and the text message below to complete both worksheets.

   (i) Print one copy of the **Excursions** worksheet in value view with gridlines only, and one copy in formula view with gridlines, and row and column headings.

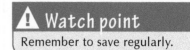

Great news!
We have been awarded a grant of **£4000** towards our excursion!

   (ii) Print one copy of the **Cost** worksheet in value view with gridlines only, and one copy in formula view with gridlines, and row and column headings.

   (b) Create a pie chart to show the percentage cost of each item of expenditure for the Barcelona excursion. Include labels on each segment and insert an appropriate heading. Print the chart on a separate sheet.

2. Download the file *SS EP2* from the Leckie and Leckie website.

   Westwood Events needs to hire cars and a coach for a corporate event.

   (a) Open the spreadsheet file and use the information in it to complete both worksheets.

   (i) Print one copy of the **Prices** worksheet in value view with gridlines only, and one copy in formula view with gridlines, and row and column headings.

   (ii) Print one copy of the **Comparison** worksheet in value view with gridlines only, and one copy in formula view with gridlines, and row and column headings.

   (b) Create a bar chart to show the discounted total cost for each hire company. Insert an appropriate heading. Print the chart on a separate sheet.

(continued)

3. Download the file *SS EP3* from the Leckie and Leckie website.

Use the information in the spreadsheet file to complete both worksheets.

(a) Print one copy of the **Costs** worksheet in value view with gridlines only, and one copy in formula view with gridlines, and row and column headings.

(b) Print one copy of the **Statement** worksheet in value view with gridlines only, and one copy in formula view with gridlines, and row and column headings.

Skill

- Literacy
- Numeracy
- Employability
- Skills for learning, life and work

Learning Checklist

Skills, knowledge and understanding	Strength ☺	☺	Weakness ☹	Next steps
Creating, editing and formatting a workbook				
I can create, edit and format a workbook: • inserting and deleting rows/columns • hiding rows/columns • alignment of data, such as centre within cell, text direction • different fonts, styles and sizes • currency, number, percentage to specified decimal places • date format • borders and shading				– Refer to instructions – Complete additional tasks – Ask teacher for help
Applying advanced functions and formulae to a workbook				
I can apply advanced functions and formulae to a workbook using: • +/–/÷/× • sum • average • maximum • minimum • count and counta • IF • link cells within worksheets • use named cells • relative and absolute cell references • sort data vertically on one or two columns				– Refer to instructions – Complete additional tasks – Ask teacher for help

Using comments

I can use comments: • add • action • delete				– Refer to instructions – Complete additional tasks – Ask teacher for help

Creating a chart and labelling it independently, using data from adjacent and non-adjacent columns and rows

I can create a chart and label it independently, using data from adjacent and non-adjacent columns and rows: • pie chart • bar (or column) chart • line graph				– Refer to instructions – Complete additional tasks – Ask teacher for help

Labelling charts meaningfully, eg:

I can label charts meaningfully, eg • Chart title • Axis labels • Data labels • Legend				– Refer to instructions – Complete additional tasks – Ask teacher for help

Printing worksheets and extracts of worksheets:

I can print worksheets and extracts of worksheets, eg • Showing value view • Showing formulae view • With and without gridlines • With and without row and column headings • In portrait and landscape orientation • With headers and/or footers, both manual and custom • To fit on one page				– Refer to instructions – Complete additional tasks – Ask teacher for help

Printing charts:

I can print charts: • Embedded in worksheets or presented separately • With identifiable labels either by colour labelling or patterns (when using black and white charts)				– Refer to instructions – Complete additional tasks – Ask teacher for help

12 Presentations

In this chapter you will learn about:

- The functions of multimedia applications to create and edit presentations.
- How to print presentations in different formats.

Use of multimedia applications

Presentations are used to pass information to an audience. For example, a Training Officer may deliver induction training to new employees and a Sales Manager may deliver a presentation on the sales targets to Sales Representatives. It is essential that the presenter creates a good impression, and that the presentation is readable, interesting and easy to understand. A variety of equipment/software can be used to prepare and present information.

Software

- **Presentation software** (such as Microsoft PowerPoint®) – used to prepare slides that can contain text, graphics, sound, animation. This can be set up to be shown automatically to the audience or the pace can be controlled by only moving on to the next slide when appropriate, allowing for discussion to take place. This software would be used with a multimedia/data projector. Printed handouts can also be produced.

- **Word-processing/DTP software** (such as Microsoft Word/Publisher®) – used to prepare handouts to accompany a presentation, which can be referred to at a later date. Text and graphics can be included.

- **Spreadsheet software** (such as Microsoft Excel®) – used to prepare graphs/charts that can be included in a handout or displayed on screen when connected to a multimedia/data projector.

Equipment

- **Multimedia/data projector** – allows images on the computer to be displayed on a large screen. Any file created on the computer can be seen by the audience, for example charts/graphs created using spreadsheet software.

- **Interactive whiteboard** – this allows data to be displayed to the audience, which can be edited/changed during the presentation.

> **⚠ Watch point**
>
> You may be asked to produce a presentation in other subjects. Remember that using presentation software will allow you to present information – including graphics, movies and sounds – in a way that is more interesting for your audience.

Advantages of using presentation software

- Information can be formatted to emphasise important information.

- Presentation can be delivered at a pace to suit the audience (using the animation function), allowing for discussion to take place.

- Slides can be created/edited very quickly for a different audience.

- Information from other applications can also be included in the presentation (graphs/charts created in a spreadsheet package).

- Printed handouts can accompany a presentation (so audience can refer back in their own time).

Functions of presentation software

Many of the skills learned in word-processing can also be used when working with presentation software.

Insert, edit, delete and format text

Text can be inserted, deleted and easily edited. Text can be formatted using different fonts, sizes and styles.

Align text

Text on the slide can be aligned – left aligned, centred, right-aligned or fully justified.

Insert and delete graphics

Graphics can be inserted – this can be done using Clipart or from a picture that has been scanned, downloaded from the Internet or uploaded from a digital camera. Graphics help to make the presentation more interesting for the audience. Graphics can be deleted by selecting them and pressing the Delete key.

Bullets and numbers

Bulleted lists are useful when presenting information, and presentation software allows the user to reveal one line of bulleted text at a time. Bullets can be shown using a variety of symbols or using numbers/letters. For example:

❑ bullets ❑ using ❑ symbols	• bullets • using • symbols	➤ bullets ➤ using ➤ symbols	✓ bullets ✓ using ✓ symbols
1 bullets 2 using 3 numbers	1) bullets 2) using 3) numbers	A. bullets B. using C. letters	a) bullets b) using c) letters

Create chart(s) and/or table(s)

Charts and tables can be included in the presentation. Most presentation software will allow the chart or table to be created in the presentation rather than in another program.

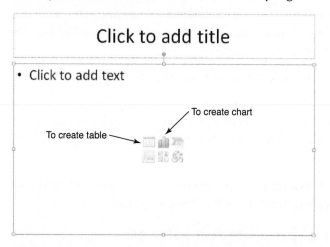

However, it is also possible, using integrated software, to copy and paste a chart or table made in another software package, for example a spreadsheet or word processed document (see below).

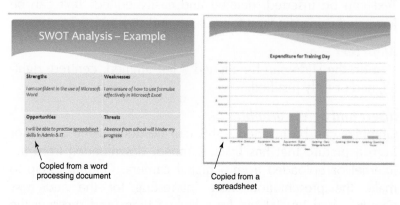

Copied from a word processing document

Copied from a spreadsheet

Add and delete slides

Current slide

When a slideshow presentation is being prepared it is usual for the current slide to be shown to the right-hand side of the screen and the order of the slides to be shown in a smaller format to the left. Every time a new slide is added/created it will appear at the end of the presentation to become the next slide. If you want to change the order it is possible to use a function (in Microsoft PowerPoint this is called 'Slide Sorter') to allow you to sort the slides into any order you wish. To delete a slide you can simply select the appropriate slide and choose delete from the appropriate menu or press the Delete key.

⚠ Watch point

Whenever you add a new slide you must ensure that the layout is consistent with the existing slides. For example, check the orientation of graphics, capitalisation of headings, style of bullets etc.

Animating text/objects

One of the advantages of using presentation software is the use of **animation** to make a presentation more interesting for the audience. This allows the user to set the text/objects to appear on screen at the click of the mouse button/keyboard key. Text and objects can appear on screen in a variety of different ways, for example they can be set to fly in (from the bottom, left, etc) or fade in. It is also possible to animate text/objects for emphasis and to exit the slide. Examples of animation:

⚠ Watch point

Do not use too many different animations on one slide as this can be distracting for the audience.

⚠ Watch point

Animations/transitions cannot be seen on a printout and so you will not be asked to do this in the Assignment.

None

Appear

Fade

Fly In

Float In

Importing data from other applications/Internet

Like any other package it is possible to use the copy and paste function to copy text/objects from another package into a presentation. Likewise, it is possible to find appropriate text and objects from the Internet and to copy these into the presentation.

Change slide layout

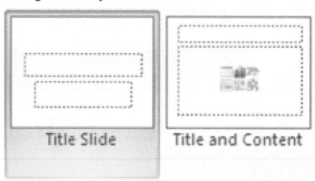

A presentation will usually start with a title slide, showing an appropriate title (and subtitle). There is a range of different slide layouts that can be used to vary the slides to suit the information. The example shown above would allow the user to insert a title for the slide and then insert text (usually in the form of a bulleted list), graphics (from Clipart or file), chart or table.

Apply slide transitions

A slide transition can be set up to allow the change from one slide to the next to be more interesting for the audience. For example, the first slide may fade away and the next slide will be revealed slowly or quickly.

Change slide order

There will be a function of the presentation software (in Microsoft PowerPoint it is called Slide Sorter) which will allow the user to drag and drop the slides to new positions.

Apply and change background, colour scheme and/or apply design templates

Slides in the presentation (all or selected) can be given a background colour or a colour scheme, often to match the content of the presentation. For example, if you were asked to create a presentation about your school you could choose a background colour or a colour scheme that reflects the colour of your school tie. The background colour of each slide could match with the main colour in the tie and the titles and text content could match with a different colour.

It is also possible to create your own background using a picture or photograph.

Presentation software usually comes with design templates that allow a user to choose a design rather than create one. It is possible to edit the colours of the design to personalise it. Examples of design templates:

⚠ Watch point

Choose **one** slide transition style – too many variations will not improve the presentation!

Insert footer on slides and handout

Footers can be added to a presentation in the same way that they can be added to a word-processed document. Footers can be used to display dates, slide numbers or an appropriate graphic, such as a company logo. Footers can be inserted on to Slides and Notes and Handouts.

Insert and delete action buttons

Action buttons are built-in shapes that can be added to the presentation to make an action occur when the mouse is clicked or moved over the button. Actions include move to the next slide, move to the previous slide, return to the first slide; and the buttons are designed to look like the action they carry out.

Insert slide and page numbers

Slide numbers can be inserted using the appropriate function (in Microsoft PowerPoint® this can be found on the Insert tab). You are then able to specify whether the page number is to be inserted on each slide or on the Notes and Handout.

Insert both specific and automatic date

The date/time can be inserted (automatically) using the appropriate function (in Microsoft PowerPoint® this can be found on the Insert tab). You are then able to specify whether the date/time is to be inserted on each slide or on the Notes and Handout. A footer or the slide master can be used if a specific date is to be inserted on each slide.

Slide master

Master slides are used to set the layout and standard formatting on **all** slides in the presentation. The placeholders (for example the title box), the objects and the formatting (font size, style etc) on the master slides are automatically applied to every slide in the presentation.

The title slide master will contain the placeholders for the presentation title (and subtitle).

Click to edit Master title style

Click to edit Master subtitle style

⚠ Watch point

Anything added to a footer must be clearly visible, in the same place on every slide and not covering any existing text.

⚠ Watch point

Always use the Action Button function to create/draw an action button. Do not just draw arrows.

⚠ Watch point

If an exam question asks you to place a slide number in a specific place, such as bottom left, then you need to think about the slide design. Some designs will place the slide numbers at the top or even down the side. Always check that the slide number is clearly visible on every slide.

The slide master will contain the placeholders for the slide title, bullet points, action buttons, etc. Any changes made to the slide master can be saved as a template. This will ensure that all slides in the presentation are the same.

Click to edit Master title style

- Click to edit Master text styles
  - Second level
    - Third level
      - Fourth level
        » Fifth level

11/11/2012   Footer

Print presentation in slide and handout format

It may be necessary to print a copy of the presentation for the presenter or the audience to refer to during the presentation (or for the audience to look at in their own time).

A presentation can be printed in slide or handout format.

Slide format will produce a copy of the presentation with one slide printed on one page. It is possible to print selected slides as well as the full presentation.

Handout format will produce a copy of the presentation with multiple slides on one page. The number of slides per page can be selected before printing. Depending on the number of slides chosen, space may be available at the side for making notes.

GO! Practice task 1

Prepare a presentation that could be used to provide induction training for new employees. The presentation should include information relating to the features of customer service and the benefits of good customer service. Your presentation should not contain more than six slides. Create a presentation using your theory knowledge and the information below.

1. Insert a title slide.
2. Apply a suitable design template.
3. Insert appropriate text and graphics on all slides.
4. Insert action buttons and slide numbers on every slide.
5. Print one copy of the presentation as a handout on one page.
6. Print one copy of only the slides on the benefits of good customer service (as full slides).

GO! Practice task 2

Download the file Presentations PT2 from the Leckie and Leckie website.

Your Head Teacher is planning to give an introductory presentation to parents about the ski trip to Neukirchen, Austria, which will take place in the last week of January next year (starting on a Saturday). Update the file Presentations PT2 following the instructions below.

1. Insert a title slide showing the name of your own school, the dates of the trip and Neukirchen Ski Trip – Introduction.

2. Number every slide and show your school logo in the top left corner.

3. Search the Internet for images of the village and ski area and insert as appropriate.

4. Apply a suitable design template.

5. Print one copy of the presentation as a handout on one page.

★ Exam practice

1. Download the folder *Presentations EP1* from the Leckie and Leckie website.

   A presentation about music venues in Scotland is to be shown to a group of music agents.

   Update the file Presentations EP1 presentation in the file using the information following the instructions below.

🌳 Skill

- Literacy
- Numeracy
- Employability
- Skills for learning, life and work

Print one copy of the presentation as a handout on one page

Insert a title slide –

MUSIC VENUES IN SCOTLAND

LIVE MUSIC AT ITS BEST

THE BARROWLANDS, GLASGOW

THE SSE HYDRO, GLASGOW

MUSIC VENUES IN SCOTLAND

We believe that nothing beats being able to see your favourite musician live and Scotland has a great choice of music venues – from small and intimate venues to massive stadiums – Scotland has it all!

Scotland has a reputation for being able to do live music like no-one else! It's no secret that Scottish audiences have been recognised by some of the world's top musicians as being among the best in the world.

Create two new slides using the same layout as slides 2 and 3. Search the Internet for images of two more Scottish music venues and insert these images on the new slides.

1 Insert the music venue's logo and slide number on every slide
2 Insert action buttons
3 Apply a suitable design template to all slides

2. Download the folder *Presentations EP2* from the Leckie and Leckie website.

Complete the task as shown below.

- Change the order of slides 2 and 3.

- Remove the action buttons and insert slide numbers and the book club logo on all slides.

- Action the comments in the file Top 10 Books and insert into slide 4.

- Open the file Charity Donations and insert the chart into slide 5.

- Apply an appropriate design and insert today's date in the footer on all slides.

- Create a final slide with the heading OUR FOUNDER.

- Key in the following information: Emma is now a well-renowned journalist with one of the national newspapers. She never forgets her early days in the Book Club and comes back to visit members regularly.

- Print one copy of the presentation as a handout on one page.

Learning Checklist

Skills, knowledge and understanding	Strength ☺		Weakness ☹	Next steps
Using the functions of multimedia applications to create and edit presentations				
I can use the functions of multimedia applications to create and edit presentations: • insert, delete and edit text • format text • insert and delete a graphic • bullets and numbers • create charts and/or tables • add and delete a slide • animate text and/or objects • import data • change slide layout • apply slide transitions • change slide order • apply and change background, colour scheme and/or apply design templates • insert footer on slides and handout • insert and delete action buttons • insert slide and page numbers • insert both specific and automatic date • use slide master				– Refer to instructions – Complete additional tasks – Ask teacher for help
Printing presentations in different formats				
I can print presentations in different formats: • slide • handout				– Refer to instructions – Complete additional tasks – Ask teacher for help

13 Electronic communication

In this chapter you will learn about:

- Searching for, extract and download relevant information from the Internet and Intranet.
- Using e-mail.
- Using an electronic diary.

Searching for and extracting/downloading relevant information

A **web browser** is a software application used to access, retrieve and view information on the Internet.

To access information on the Internet, a website address (also known as a Uniform Resource Locator – **URL**) can be keyed in, or, if the user is unsure of the website address then keywords can be typed into a **search engine**.

A search engine makes it possible to find a specific item of information from the vast amount of data stored on the web. To use a search engine you type in the words that describe the information you are interested in and a (usually) long list of pages that contain related content will appear. Examples of search engines include Google, Yahoo!, Bing and Ask.

Once you either key in the website address or choose from the list displayed by the search engine, the **homepage** of the website is usually displayed. The homepage is the first page you see on a website and will often have general information about the company, its history, products and contents of the website. The home page will usually contain a **search box** – this allows the user to type in keywords to find relevant information contained *within* the website.

Most websites contain **hyperlinks**, which allow the user to go from one part of the website to another. When you move your mouse over the hyperlink it usually changes from an arrow to a hand and the link becomes underlined.

⚠ **Watch point**

Material downloaded from the Internet may be subject to copyright law.

Information from a website can be **downloaded** onto an individual's computer. Usually it is better to copy the text required and paste it to a word/presentation document (omitting adverts, pictures etc) before printing.

Bookmarks/Favourites allow the user to store the addresses of frequently visited websites. This avoids wasting time either keying in the website address in full each time, or using a search engine.

Using e-mail

In order to be able to use e-mail, an account must be set up. E-mail addresses usually follow the same format, for example: username@companyname.co.uk

For the purpose of this course you should be able to:

1. Access your e-mail account and compose a message to be sent to one or more recipients (you will need the recipient's e-mail address).

2. Receive an e-mail and reply to it using the reply function (this saves you keying in the recipient's e-mail address).

3. Use the forward function.

4. Use cc to copy other recipients into the e-mail.

5. Identify e-mail messages that are urgent and mark them as high priority.

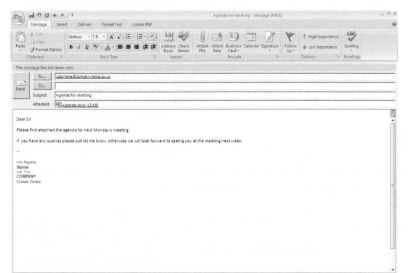

> ⚠ **Watch point**
> You will lose a keyboarding mark if you include a comma after the opening remark.

6. Use the address book facility. Using the address book saves time and effort when trying to remember different people's e-mail addresses (they are usually quite long and can be complicated).

7. Add an attachment.

8. Create a signature to make your e-mail look more personal.

In order to obtain full marks for an e-mail task you should:

*   Include an appropriate subject heading (not simply the task number).

*   Include an opening remark, such as Hi, Hello, Good morning etc.

*   Ensure your message makes sense, is grammatically accurate, includes the correct information and ends with a full stop.

- Include a closing remark, such as Regards, Kind regards, etc, followed by your full name.

- Check if any files have to be attached and ensure the correct file is attached to the e-mail (the marker will check the type of file to make sure you have attached the correct file).

- Check to see if the e-mail has to be marked as urgent and mark as urgent or high priority if necessary.

- **Never** use text speak or emoticons in an e-mail.

> ⚠️ **Watch point**
>
> Marks can be easily lost in the e-mail for capitalisation errors – always proofread your work carefully to ensure capitals are being used appropriately.

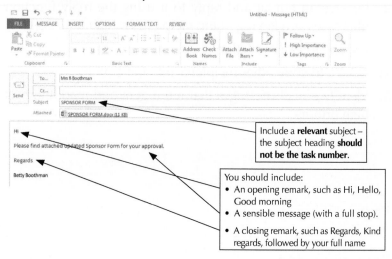

Include a **relevant** subject – the subject heading **should not be the task number**.

You should include:
- An opening remark, such as Hi, Hello, Good morning
- A sensible message (with a full stop).
- A closing remark, such as Regards, Kind regards, followed by your full name

You will be expected to print evidence to show you have sent the e-mail. To do this, go to your sent items, open the e-mail and print a copy of the message from the sent items.

Wed 04/10/2017 11:10

Mrs B Boothman

RE: SPONSOR FORM

To   Mrs B Boothman

The date and time of sending the e-mail will be shown when you open the e-mail from your sent items. The examiner will look for this in order to award the 'evidence of sending' mark.

Sending a reply

The examiner will know that you have used the reply function as your subject line will say RE: and/or your original message will be displayed.

Electronic diary (e-diary)

For the purpose of this course you should be able to:

1. Enter an appointment – date, time, duration and location of meeting.

2. Enter a recurring meeting.

3. Set a reminder.

4. Print the calendar in daily, weekly and monthly view.

5. Create a to-do list (task).

6. Access other users' calendars.

In order to obtain full marks for an e-diary task you should:

- Ensure the start and finish times of meetings/events are shown clearly on the printout.

- Ensure all text is visible. If text is truncated (cut off and cannot be seen) you must amend the printing style to ensure all text is visible. You may include additional printouts if necessary.

- Check your spelling and capitalisation. It is a good idea to copy the text from the question exactly as it is shown, for example using the same capital letters.

- Check if the location is required. If not, leave the location blank as you will lose a keyboarding mark if you insert the location with a keyboarding error.

- Check how the e-diary has to be printed. You may be asked to print the day view, 5-day-week view, 7-day-week view or month view.

- Ensure reminders show all event details (without truncation) and the reminder time setting.

- Enter tasks in a task manager (not simply in the e-diary). Tasks must clearly show the day for completion.

> **⚠ Watch point**
>
> Your teacher will give you specific instructions for using the software in your school to complete Internet, e-mail and e-diary tasks.

GO! Practice task 1

You are an administrator in your local high school. You have been given the task of organising the S5/6 prom. You receive the following e-mail from the organising committee.

> To: Administrator
>
> From: Kirstin Dolan, School Captain
>
> Subject: Our Prom!!!
>
> We are all so excited about the prom on 14 June this year.
>
> We are unsure about a venue – can you find information on **two** venue/hotels that would be willing to host a prom? I think there will be approximately 100 people attending. We are happy to travel approximately 5 miles from school.
>
> Can you find out the names of **two** local bus companies?
>
> Print out the information we require.
>
> Thanks
> Kirstin

GO! Practice task 2

On the first Monday of next month, the Sales Manager will be involved in various meetings regarding a new advertising campaign. She has asked to you provide admin support at all of these meetings.

1. Update your e-diary with all the following information:

Monday		
9 am–9.30 am	Meeting with Managing Director	Head Office
1.00 pm–2.00 pm	Lunch with advertising agency staff	Buchanan Centre, Glasgow
3.45 pm	Conference call with Bright Marketing Consultants (1 hour)	
Wednesday/Thursday/Friday		
4.30 pm–5.00 pm	Staff Meeting	Meeting Room 1

Set a reminder half an hour before the meeting with the Managing Director.

Task (Tuesday) – Photocopy training manuals to be issued at staff meeting.

2. Print in week view (work week only).

GO! Practice task 3

Complete the following exercise.

To: Administrator

From: lucynewlands@yha.com

Date: Today's

Subject: SALES CONFERENCE IN O2 ARENA, LONDON

I wish to travel from Glasgow to London Heathrow on the first Tuesday of next month (after 6 pm) and return on Thursday (of the same week) before 10 am.

I will require accommodation in London and I would like to stay in a 4 or 5 star hotel. Could you also find out the nearest London Underground station to the O2 arena?

Part A
Use the Internet to research the required information. Print one copy of the relevant information.

Part B
E-mail the relevant information to me (you should have a note of my e-mail address) – please do not book as I wish to check it over and then confirm the flights, accommodation arrangements before booking. Print one copy of the sent e-mail.

Part C
Please enter the sales conference into my e-diary as an all day event on Wednesday. Print one copy in daily view.

Skill

- Literacy
- Numeracy
- Employability
- Skills for learning, life and work

⚠ Watch point

Do not confuse star reviews with star ratings. If the question asks for 4-star accommodation this does not mean a rating from a review website. It is a rating awarded by either The AA, Visit Britain, Visit Scotland or Visit Wales.

★ Exam practice

Complete the following:

1.
> To: Administrator
>
> From: Carly Lavery
>
> Date: Today's
>
> Subject: LUNCH AND OVERNIGHT IN EDINBURGH
>
> I will be meeting a client in Edinburgh on (first Wednesday of next month) to discuss an upcoming event. I require information on a 4-star review lunch venue and a 4-star hotel in the city.
>
> I will be travelling by car to the lunch venue in Edinburgh from Motherwell (ML1 2QN) and require driving directions and how long it will take to drive.
>
> Before I attend the meeting I must investigate different venues for a wedding in Edinburgh – please include this as a task in my e-diary on the day before the meeting.
>
> Assuming I will go to the restaurant you have selected for a lunch meeting lasting 2 hours, insert the relevant information in my e-diary and print a copy in weekly view.

2.
> Hi
>
> I wish to attend a meeting with a client on (second Monday of next month) at 10.30 am in Wishaw. The meeting is expected to last 2 hours.
>
> Search the Internet to find times of direct trains to and from Glasgow to Wishaw. It will take 15 minutes to walk from the train station to the meeting venue and I will require a return ticket. Find out the cost of a return ticket.
>
> Print the relevant information.
>
> Insert the relevant information in my e-dairy. Please set a reminder one hour before the train departs for Wishaw. Print this in daily view.
>
> Thanks
>
> Amelia

Learning Checklist

Skills, knowledge and understanding	Strength ☺	☺	Weakness ☹	Next steps
Searching for, extracting and downloading relevant information from the Internet and Intranet				
I can search for, extract and download relevant information from the Internet and Intranet • opening browser • using search engines • navigating hyperlinks • copying information from a web page to a word-processing/DTP document and presentation • using favourites/bookmarks • printing information and/or an extract of information				– Refer to instructions – Complete additional tasks – Ask teacher for help
Using e-mail				
I can use e-mail: • composing e-mail by entering text and sending to one or more recipients • using the address book facility • marking urgent • using cc • using reply • using forward • adding attachment(s) • creating a signature				– Refer to instructions – Complete additional tasks – Ask teacher for help
Using an e-diary				
I can use an e-diary: • scheduling appointment • setting reminder • printing calendar: day, week and month view • scheduling recurring appointments • accessing other users' calendars • scheduling tasks				– Refer to instructions – Complete additional tasks – Ask teacher for help

Preparing for the Assignment and Question Paper

> ⚠ **Watch point**
>
> In order to fully prepare for the Assignment you should attempt as many previous assignments as possible – remember Admin & IT is a skill-based subject and you only get better at it if you practise as much as you can. You will find past examples on the SQA website – www.sqa.org.uk

The Assignment

The assignment is worth 70 marks.

You will work through a series of planning, support and follow-up tasks related to an event or business.

You will complete the assignment over a 3 hour period – how this is conducted and the date(s) on which it will be attempted will be decided by your centre. Your teacher will provide you with the relevant information. The assignment is a closed-book assessment, this means that you will have no access to any resources, previous work, teacher guidance etc while attempting it. The assignment is externally assessed.

Marking is always positive. This means that, for each of your responses, marks are accumulated for the demonstration of relevant skills, knowledge and understanding: they are not deducted on the basis of errors or omissions. Marks will be awarded for demonstrating skills in the use of the different IT applications.

The following gives a breakdown of the different skills being assessed and examples of what might be contained with the tasks. Reminders of dos and don'ts are also provided.

> ⚠ **Watch point**
>
> Additional advice on WP/DTP formatting eg dates, time is given on page 72

Word-processing/DTP: 30 marks (+/–3 marks)

- Entering and editing text
    - all text entered must be consistent with house style and any existing text
    - all text entered must be accurate
    - manuscript correction instructions must be carried out
- Layout and presentation of information
    - letters – house style must be followed, appropriate reference (person signing letter's initials/own initials), date (in full, including year), appropriate subject heading, complimentary close (Dear Mr/Mrs … Yours sincerely, Dear Sir/Madam … Yours faithfully)
    - itineraries – house style must be followed, use 24-hour clock (include the word 'hours', such as

1300 hours), use an appropriate heading, dates must include the year

- forms – make full use of the page, use a variety of fonts/styles/sizes, graphic(s), shading

- agendas/minutes of meetings – follow the layout given, date must include the year, time must include am/pm or hours (if using 24-hour clock)

- templates can be used to create business cards, with compliments slips, newsletters, certificates, posters/notices

- size appropriately – business card 8·75 cm x 5 cm, name badge 8·75 cm x 5 cm, with compliments slip 21 cm x 10 cm, posters/notices/newsletters full page

- use a variety of fonts/styles/sizes/graphic(s)

- Key information included

- full contact details should include address/telephone number/(fax number)/e-mail address/web address

- all information must be visible

Communication: 30 marks (+/–3 marks)

- Entering text

- all text entered must be consistent with any existing text

- all text entered must be accurate

- Key information included

- presentations – should be able to insert new slides (with appropriate layouts), insert action buttons, apply an appropriate design, insert slide numbers, print in handout format

- e-mail – must include an appropriate subject heading, an opening ('Hi'), content (in sentences that make sense), a close ('Thanks' or 'Regards'), own name, Urgent label should be used for high priority, cc/bcc for sending to more than one person, evidence of sending must be provided

- Internet search – evidence of search results must be provided and relevant information must be highlighted

Knowledge and understanding: 10 marks (+/–3 marks)

- marks will be awarded for providing responses as part of an integrated IT task

  - text keyed in **must** be accurate (although no marks will be deducted for keying in errors)

See the separate section (at end of this chapter) on Theory revision for more information.

Layouts

Marks will be awarded for a wide variety of layouts used in word-processing and desktop publishing tasks. The overriding principle is that a document must be fit for purpose.

Printouts

You will be clearly directed, within the instructions, as to the printing requirements.

Remember: no printout will mean that no marks can be awarded!

The Question Paper

The Question Paper is worth 50 marks.

You must complete the entire closed-book Question Paper under supervised conditions in two hours. You will have to complete the Question Paper independently of your teacher. You will not have access to any previous work, shared work or the Internet. The Question Paper will be externally assessed. Your overall grade will be determined by your performance across the Assignment and the Question Paper. You will be awarded a grade from A to D.

Marking is always positive. This means that, for each of your responses, marks are accumulated for the demonstration of relevant skills, knowledge and understanding: they are not deducted from a maximum on the basis of errors or omissions. Marks will be awarded for demonstrating skills in the use of the different IT applications.

The following gives a breakdown of the different skills being assessed and examples of what might be contained with the tasks. Reminders of dos and don'ts are also provided.

Spreadsheet: 20 marks (+/–3 marks)

- creating, editing and formatting a workbook

  - all text entered must be consistent with entries already made

- all text entered must be accurate
- merge cells
- applying advanced functions and formulae to a workbook
  - simple formulae: + – * / (Never use SUM in a simple formula that only contains two cell references)
  - functions: SUM, MAX, MIN, AVERAGE, IF
  - use of absolute cell references ($ – press F4)
  - replication of formulae (dragging down/across)
  - name cells
  - link cells to another worksheet
- using comments
  - all comments must be deleted once actioned
- creating a chart using data from adjacent and non-adjacent columns and rows
  - when printing a chart in black and white, you must remember to choose the black and white option in Page Setup if not printing to colour printer
- labelling charts meaningfully
  - this may include showing the labels on the chart (as % or value)
- printing worksheets, extracts of worksheets and charts (embedded in worksheets or separately – a value and formulae printout must be provided)
  - spreadsheets must clearly show all information and be printed on one page

Database: 20 marks (+/–3 marks)

- creating forms, reports and labels
  - create a form (using more than one table) – to include appropriate heading
  - create a report from a query – to include appropriate heading/graphic(s)
- editing a relational database using tables and forms
  - all text entered must be consistent with entries already made
  - all text entered must be accurate
  - insert new field(s), formatted appropriately

- searching information in a relational database
    - create a complex query – search on more than one field
- sorting information in a relational database
    - create a complex query – sort on more than one field
- printing
    - print selected form(s) only
    - print selected field(s) only – as a query/report on one page

Theory: 10 marks (+/–3 marks)

- marks will be awarded for providing responses as part of an integrated IT task
    - text keyed in **must** be accurate (although no marks will be deducted for keying in errors)

See the separate section (at end of this chapter) on Theory revision for more information.

Printouts

You will be clearly directed, within the instructions, as to the printing requirements. All database and spreadsheet tasks **must** be printed on one page.

Remember: no printout will mean that no marks can be awarded!

Points to consider across all tasks (Assignment and Question Paper)

- All dates must be shown in full – the year must be included and you must make sure that every date included within a task is entered in the same way.
- Names must include title, first name, surname (separate fields must be used in a database).
- Addresses must include street, town, postcode (separate fields must be used in a database).
- Ensure that graphics do not cover any text and/or that graphics are not clipped by the margin.
- All data/text must be visible – ensure that fields in databases/columns in spreadsheets are wide enough.
- Capital letters must be used for proper nouns. At all other times capitalisation must be consistent, such as using the same capitalisation as field/row/column headings already

given. Small words (conjunctions) do not require capitalisation (even as part of a heading), such as Administration and IT.

- Headings must always be enhanced – in capital letters, in bold, underlined. Follow the format of the capitalisation already provided.

- If abbreviations are used, such as tel no, you must be consistent, such as fax no.

- Always be consistent with spacing between sentences and paragraphs.

- Never use text speak or emoticons.

- Printing – follow printing instructions.

- PowerPoint – it is normal practice to print this as a handout (to fit one page).

- Mail merge – it is normal practice to print out a copy showing the merged fields and also a copy of a merged document (this may be to only one recipient).

- Spreadsheets – it is normal practice to print both a value and a formula printout.

- When printing spreadsheets and databases you must print on only one page.

- Inserting footers – you must insert your own name/task as a footer and this must appear below any other footer information you have been asked to insert.

- When you have finished your Assignment/Question Paper you must proofread every task. You must put tasks in the correct order before placing into the plastic pocket.

Theory revision

For the theory element of the course, you are introduced to the responsibilities of organisations, the skills/qualities and tasks (duties) of the administrative support function, and the impact of these in the workplace.

Administration theory in the workplace covers the following:

- Tasks (duties) of administrators.

- Skills/qualities of administrators.

- Customer service: features, benefits and consequences.

- Health and safety: features of current legislation and organisational responsibilities.

- Security of people, property and information: organisational responsibilities and features of current legislation.

- Sources of information from Internet: features and benefits of reliable Internet sources and consequences of unreliable Internet sources.

- File management: features, benefits of good file management and consequences of poor file management.

- Corporate image: features, benefits of having a corporate image and consequences of not having a corporate image or having a bad corporate image.

- Electronic communication: methods, features, uses and benefits.

Theory will be assessed in both the Assignment and the Question Paper.

- Assignment: 10–18% of the total 70 marks will be awarded for theory.

- Question Paper: 14–26% of the total 50 marks will be awarded for theory.

Sample answers to exam questions

Answering an Outline question

Outline 3 features of good file management.

- Files should be saved using relevant names.

- Files should be saved into appropriate folders.

- Files should be backed up on a regular basis.

Answering a Describe question

2017 SQA Assignment (amended)

Describe a way that Scotland Cares could use the following method of communication – e-mail

In order to gain the mark, two points would need to be made as follows:

1   2

… to contact participants (individual/group) about upcoming events.

1   2

… to contact organisations to request donations/sponsorship.

> ⚠️ **Watch point**
>
> You should make sure you expand your theory answers and take note of the command word used in the question (see page 9 for command words).

Answering an Explain question

Explain the consequences of using unreliable Internet sources of information.

You have to give the initial statement but you **must** go on to give the consequence of this (what happens as a result of using an unreliable website). For example:

- Unreliable sources may give inaccurate information, *meaning* the wrong decision is made.

- Unreliable sources may be out of date, *meaning* a decision that should have been made if the information had been received on time is missed. This could result in a lost opportunity.

2017 SQA Assignment (amended)

Explain qualities/skills an Administrator should have.

In order to gain the mark, two points would need to be made as follows:

1　　　　　　　　　　　　　**2**

… be reliable/responsible/hard working to ensure all tasks are completed on time.

Answers must relate to employer/organisation responsibilities

At National 5 **all** answers should relate to employer/organisation responsibilities. You might not be told this in the question but you should know to do this. Start your answer with 'The organisation/employer should/must …' where appropriate. Alternatively, include the organisation name in your answer, 'Scotland Cares should/must …', for example.

Describe methods of ensuring the security of property.

You must describe the organisational responsibilities:

- **Organisations/employers must** provide lockers or lockable drawers for employees to keep their personal items in.

- **Organisations/employers must** have a policy that staff should lock their offices at the end of the day or employ security staff to check all rooms are locked at night.

When legislation is assessed you must ensure that answers are relevant to an office environment, such as:

- Health and Safety at Work Act 1974

- Health and Safety (Display Screen Equipment) Regulations 1992

- Health and Safety (First Aid) Regulations 1981

- Fire Precautions (Place of Work) Regulations 1995

Answers

Chapter 1

Theory questions

1. Two from:

   - The administrator will answer the phone politely at all times and deal with any enquiries.

   - The administrator will create and update databases containing records about employees, customers or even suppliers.

   - The administrator will send and receive e-mails to customers and suppliers on behalf of the organisation.

   - The administrator will make/update diary appointments to ensure that there are no double bookings.

   - Working on reception – the administrator may have to work on the reception desk and deal with visitors, making sure that visitors sign in and out and are issued with badges.

   - The administrator will file documents, both paper and electronic. This means keeping files in an order so that they can be found again easily.

2. Two from:

   - The administrator should have good IT skills – **as** their job requires them to use spreadsheets, databases and word-processing software, and to send and receive e-mails.

   - The administrator should be well organised – **as** they will be dealing with lots of information and need to be able to make sure they can find it again at a later date.

   - The administrator will be keen to learn – **as** IT skills constantly need updating and they should be enthusiastic about learning new skills.

   - The administrator will need good communication skills – **as** they will be dealing with enquiries from customers and staff by phone and e-mail. They will need to be clear and polite at all times.

3. A job description is used to provide an applicant with the tasks/duties that will they will be required to carry out. An applicant can then decide if this job would suit them before applying.

4. A person specification is used to provide an applicant with the skills/qualities that they should have to be able to carry out the job. These may be listed as essential or desirable. An applicant can then decide if they have the appropriate skills/qualities before applying.

Chapter 2

Theory questions

1. Three from:

   - Communicating with customers – answering calls received by customers promptly and not leaving them on hold for a long period of time.

   - Ensuring a high quality of customer service – providing regular customer service training for employees.

   - Monitoring customer satisfaction – carrying out surveys, using loyalty cards etc.

   - Dealing with customer complaints effectively – keeping customers informed of what is happening when they have a problem. For example, if we promise to call you back, we will do this, even if to say we are still looking into things.

2. Three from:

   - Satisfied customers, leading to a reduction in complaints.

   - Satisfied customers will become loyal and keep returning.

   - Satisfied customers will tell others of their experience, leading to a good reputation.

   - A good reputation will encourage new customers.

   - Increased customers (loyal and new) will lead to an increase in sales/profits/market share.

   - Staff morale will improve, leading to reduced absenteeism/lower rate of staff turnover/reduced (recruitment) costs.

3. Three from:

   - Dissatisfied customers will lead to more complaints.

   - Dissatisfied customers will go elsewhere (to competitors) which means sales will fall.

   - Dissatisfied customers will tell others of their experience, leading to a poor reputation (this is very difficult to turn around).

- A poor reputation will not encourage new customers.

- A fall in the number of customers will lead to a decrease in sales/profits/market share.

- Staff morale will be low, leading to increased absenteeism/ higher rate of staff turnover/increased (recruitment) costs.

Chapter 3

Theory questions

1. **(a)** Two from: trailing cables; open filing cabinet; person standing on chair; fire exit blocked.

   (b) Two from: chair that is not adjustable; glare on computer screen from window with no blind; pain in wrist caused by repetitive strain injury.

2. Training given to **new** employees to introduce them to the organisation. It usually focuses on the organisation's policies and procedures, such as health and safety.

3.

Responsibilities of Employee	Responsibilities of Organisation
Employees should take reasonable care of their own health and safety and the health and safety of others.	Employers/organisations should provide and maintain suitable surroundings for employees such as lighting, workstations etc.
Employees should Co-operate with the employer on health and safety matters.	Employers/organisations should provide information and training on all health and safety matters and requirements and ensure that employees adhere to these.
Employees should not misuse or interfere with anything provided for employees' health and safety.	Employers/organisations should provide protective clothing and equipment, if necessary, and make sure that all equipment and machinery is checked and tested on a regular basis.
Employees should report any accidents or hazards immediately to their employer.	Employers/organisations should prepare a health and safety policy to be given to all employees and update it on a regular basis.
	Employers/organisations should ensure an accident report form and accident book are kept and maintained. The employer should also make sure staff are aware that all accidents/incidents are to be recorded by including this in induction training/notices etc.

4.

Responsibilities of an employee	Responsibilities of an employer (organisation)
Employees should avoid potential health hazards by: • Making use of adjustment facilities for the VDU. • Adjusting chair for maximum comfort. • Arranging desk and screen to avoid glare.	Employers/organisations should assess workstation requirements: • Employers/organisations should provide adjustable seating. • Employers/organisations should provide adjustable and tilting screens. • Employers/organisations should provide health and safety training for employees. • Employers/organisations should organise daily work of VDU users so that there are regular rest breaks or changes in activity.

5. Provide a well-stocked first aid box; appoint a first aider (it is recommended that there should be one for every 50–100 employees); inform staff of first-aid procedures; keep a record of all accidents/incidents.

6. Any **two** from: assess fire risks in the organisation; provide and maintain appropriate fire-fighting equipment such as fire extinguishers; provide warning systems and check them regularly; train employees in fire procedures; regularly check evacuation procedures (regular fire drills would help check routes are appropriate, timings are acceptable etc).

Chapter 4

Theory questions

1. Access is restricted to those who are authorised and who have the appropriate number/card. Swipe cards can be programmed to allow an employee access to only the areas that they are permitted to enter. Similarly, staff may hold the number/card for only the areas they require access to and not others.

2. The organisation should install intercom/swipe cards/keypads/iris/fingerprint recognition to prevent unauthorised entry to the premises; the organisation should employ security guards to prevent unauthorised access; the organisation should install CCTV to monitor secure areas.

3. The organisation should attach equipment to desks, for example computers, keyboards etc can be bolted to desks to ensure no one can remove them from the premises; the organisation should keep a list of equipment (including serial numbers) to allow equipment to be identified. This may act as a deterrent to thieves; the organisation should provide security cables to be used with portable items such as laptops/notebooks/netbooks etc. This will secure items to ensure they cannot be removed from the premises.

4. The **computer** can only be used when the username/ password is entered correctly. A username and password provide access rights – the user can access the **files** (information) they require.

5. The organisation should have a policy to encrypt files; the organisation should train staff to put passwords on files; the organisation should ensure backups are made.

6. Main principles:

   - Lawfulness, fairness and transparency – data should be processed lawfully, fairly and in a transparent manner in relation to individuals.

   - Purpose limitation – data should be collected for specified, explicit and legitimate purposes and not further processed in a manner that is incompatible with those purposes.

   - Data minimisation – data should be adequate, relevant and limited to what is necessary in relation to the purposes for which they are processed.

   - Accuracy – data should be error-free and, where necessary, kept up to date; every reasonable step must be taken to ensure that personal data that is inaccurate is updated or deleted without delay.

   - Storage limitation – data should be kept in a form that permits identification of data subjects for no longer than is necessary for the purposes for which the personal data are processed.

   - Integrity and confidentiality – data should be processed in a manner that ensures appropriate security of the personal data, including protection against unauthorised or unlawful processing and against accidental loss, destruction or damage, using appropriate technical or organisational measures.

   - Accountability – this requires the organisation to take responsibility for what they do with personal data and how they comply with the other principles.

     An organisation must have appropriate measures and records in place to be able to demonstrate that they are complying with the GDPR.

7. The purpose of the Computer Misuse Act 1990 is to prohibit unlawful access to computer systems.

8. The purpose of the Copyright, Design and Patents Act is to ensure that no unauthorised copying takes place.

Chapter 5

Theory questions

1. **Non-biased** – using a range of websites will help achieve a balanced view before making any decisions; **complete/ sufficient** – using a range of websites should ensure a user has enough information to make an informed decision; **accurate** – users should always check information contained on a website is correct.

2. Three from: information is usually up to date, which makes decision-making more reliable; a vast range of information is available meaning the correct decision is more likely to be reached; an organisation will gain a good reputation if it provides customers with up-to-date, reliable information; if an organisation has access to up-to-date information it may be able to take advantage of special offers, which would allow it to reduce its costs; information is instantly available, for example when booking a flight a number of reputable websites could be searched for prices and availability, allowing the organisation to book the most appropriate flight. This would save the organisation time and money.

3. Using out-of-date information could have a damaging effect on the business, for example using an out-of-date train timetable could result in staff missing important meetings and thus losing orders/sales; biased information could influence search results and could lead to wrong decisions being made; if an organisation passes on unreliable information to its customers it may gain a bad reputation, which could lead to customers not using the business again in the future; using an unreliable website could also result in missed opportunities. For example, the organisation may be unaware of innovative product designs etc which customers may now demand – this could lead to losing sales.

Chapter 6

Theory questions

1. Three from:
   - Files should be saved using appropriate/meaningful names.
   - Files should be saved into appropriately named folders.
   - Files should be backed up regularly.
   - Files that are no longer required should be archived/ deleted.
   - Confidential files should be kept secure using passwords.

2. Three from:

- Employees do not have difficulty finding files, **which** saves time.

- Employees understand how files are saved, **which** reduces frustration/stress.

- Time is saved finding files, **which** leads to satisfied customers.

- Computer systems are not storing out-of-date files, **which** speeds up processing.

- All files accessed are up to date/current, **which** means that good decisions are made.

- Confidential files cannot be accessed by unauthorised personnel, **which** means that legislation is not being breached.

3. Three from:

- Time is wasted trying to find files.

- Space is wasted on the network (duplication of files).

- There is more stress for employees looking for files.

- There will be lower efficiency, leading to a poor reputation.

- Due to duplication, files are less likely to be up to date.

Chapter 7

Theory questions

1. Four from:

- Using standardised colours, fonts, graphics.

- Having an easily recognisable logo.

- Having an easily recognisable slogan.

- All employees wear an easily recognisable uniform.

- Having a similar store layout across all branches.

- Having standardised responses to FAQs.

- Using a consistent presentation of IT documents/house style.

2. Two from: policy statements; training; employing specialised staff; having an effective recruitment and selection procedure.

3. Two from:

- The organisation has an instantly recognisable brand, **which means** that customers know what to expect.

- The organisation has a more professional reputation, **which means** new customers can be attracted.

- Staff are more consistent so that customers are dealt with fairly, **which means** that loyal customers will return.

- For many companies, brand image is worth millions, **which means** the most valuable asset a company may have when being sold is not the factories it owns but the trademarks and brand image it has built up over the years.

4. Two from:

- No recognisable brand, **which can** make it difficult to attract customers.

- Less professional reputation, **which means** that new customers are not likely to be attracted.

- Staff are less consistent, **so that** customers are not dealt with fairly, which can lead to customer dissatisfaction.

Chapter 8

Theory questions

1. Three from: **A fast method of sending (urgent) information:** messages can be sent instantly to anywhere in the world. **A relatively inexpensive method of communication:** it is cheaper than making a telephone call/posting a letter. **Attachments can be sent easily:** previously prepared files such as spreadsheets, database files, letters or picture can be attached to the e-mail. **Group e-mail can be used:** one e-mail can be prepared and sent to a number of different recipients at the same time. **Messages can be flagged according to priority (high, low):** this allows the recipient to prioritise the order in which he/she opens e-mail messages. **A receipt/confirmation facility** asks the recipient to let the sender know that they have received and opened the e-mail message they sent. **Messages can be forwarded to other users:** if someone receives a message they wish to let others see, they can easily forward the e-mail to them. **Copies (cc) and blind copies (bcc) of the e-mail can be sent to a number of people:** if a bcc is used, the initial recipient will be unaware that this person has also received a copy of the e-mail. **E-mail is convenient:** e-mail allows communication at any time of the day. **Confidential information can be sent** via e-mail, as a password is required to access the e-mail. **Mailing lists can be created:** subscribers to a mailing list will receive e-mails containing relevant information on a regular basis.